The Original
John G. Lake
Devotional

The Original
John G. Lake
Devotional

Larry Keefauver
General Editor

THE ORIGINAL JOHN G. LAKE DEVOTIONAL
Published by Creation House
Strang Communications Company
600 Rinehart Road
Lake Mary, Florida 32746
Web site: http://www.creationhouse.com

Unless otherwise noted, all Scripture quotations are from the
King James Version of the Bible.

Copyright © 1997 by Creation House
Interior design by Lillian McAnally
All rights reserved
Printed in the United States of America

Library of Congress Cataloging-in-Publication Data
The Original Maria Woodworth-Etter Devotional / Larry
Keefauver, general editor.
1. Devotional calendars.   2. Christian life—Pentecostal
authors.
I. Keefauver, Larry.
ISBN: 0-88419-479-5
BV4811.L35 1997   242'.2—dc21   97-23310
78901234 RPG 87654321

Contents

Contents

Introduction

JOHN GRAHAM LAKE'S life began with the need for a healing miracle. Born in 1870 in Ontario, Canada, one of sixteen children, John Lake struggled as a child with a digestive disease that almost robbed him of life. While he did survive, eight of his brothers and sisters died. From the outset, John Lake knew that sickness and sorrow were evil attacks that only the power of God could ultimately overcome.

Lake's family moved to Michigan when he was sixteen. While there John Lake was saved in a Salvation Army meeting and joined a Methodist church. He sought God desperately desiring to learn how to break the curse of disease and death on his family.

At church, the pastor and members told

him to endure patiently while he watched his body become deformed by crippling rheumatism. Deep down inside, John Lake knew that sickness was not God's will for his life or for anyone else's for that matter. He sought God's healing at John Alexander Dowie's Divine Healing Home in Chicago. While there God's power surged through his weak and deformed body, completely straightening his limbs and healing him. John Lake had encountered what he later termed *a strong man's gospel.*

Though his earlier education had focused on engineering, at age twenty-one Lake redirected his studies to become a Methodist minister. In 1891 he married Jennie Stevens. They had seven children.

Five years after their wedding, the Lakes discovered that Jennie had tuberculosis and incurable heart disease. Lake found himself surrounded by affliction and attacks of the enemy—two of his sisters were critically ill, his brother was an invalid, and his beloved wife weakened daily.

Once again John Lake sought God's power and contacted Dowie in Chicago asking for his prayers. In the coming months both of his sisters were healed, but his dear Jennie remained deathly ill. John Lake and his wife held onto God all the more and claimed Acts 10:38, "God anointed Jesus of Nazareth with the Holy Ghost and with power: who went about doing good, and healing all that were oppressed of the devil; for God was with him."

Lake understood that the source of disease was an attack of the devil and that Jesus was with them through the power of the Holy Spirit. He came to believe that the same power of the Holy Spirit was also in him by faith in Christ through the indwelling Holy Spirit. So he called his friends and announced that at 9:30 A.M. on April 28, 1898, Jennie would be healed. At the appointed time, Lake laid his hands on his wife and immediately her paralysis left, her heart began beating normally, her breathing and temperature returned to normal, and she declared, "Praise God! I am healed!"

John Lake and his family now knew God's healing power as a reality for themselves and others. After a few years of working very successfully in business, amassing a small fortune while ministering part time, John Lake continued to cry out for more of God. For nine months in 1907, Lake fasted and prayed for the baptism of the Holy Spirit. Suddenly, the baptism fell, and Lake was filled to overflowing with God's Spirit. He became so sensitized to the Spirit that he could lay hands on people and reveal to them their illness before they ever spoke.

Lake left business and entered into a full-time evangelistic healing ministry. God led him and fellow workers to South Africa, where thousands were reached over the years for Christ, and scores were healed by the power of God. He established a main church in Johannesburg and planted over one hundred churches in surrounding areas. His staff grew to over a hundred and twenty-five ministers. But in the midst of great advances, there were many financial difficulties, and not even a year into his ministry, his beloved Jennie died while he was in Africa.

Undaunted, Lake returned to America to care for his children and to raise funds for the work in South Africa. He founded the Apostolic Faith Mission and the Zion Christian Church which grew to over six hundred congregations with a hundred thousand converts, and witnessed countless miracles by 1913.

By the end of 1913, Lake returned to America with his children and moved to Spokane, Washington. There he started a healing clinic and began training healing technicians to minister God's power to the sick.

The International Apostolic Congress, headquartered in Spokane, continued to grow worldwide under Lake's leadership. In 1920, Lake moved to Portland, Oregon, to oversee another Apostolic church. By 1924, newspapers reported John Lake as a nationally known healing evangelist with forty churches in the United States and Canada. It was also reported that Spokane, Washington, had experienced over a hundred thousand healings through Lake's ministry and was the healthiest place in American to reside.

His endless travels, crusades, church plantings, and healing clinics drained his physical strength. Still filled with vision, bold faith, and a strong man's gospel, John Lake met the Healer face-to-face in September 1935.

—LARRY KEEFAUVER, D.MIN.
GENERAL EDITOR

Day 1

The Ultimate Note

*Praise ye the Lord. Sing unto the Lord a
new song, and his praise in the congrega-
tion of saints.*

—Psalm 149:1

Musicians talk of an ultimate note. That
is a note you will not find on any key-
boards. It is a peculiar note. A man sits down
to tune a piano or any fine instrument. He has
no guide to the proper key, and yet he has a
guide. That guide is the note that he has in his
soul. And the nearer he can bring his instrument into harmony with that note in his soul,
the nearer perfection he has attained.

There is an ultimate note in the heart of the
Christian. It is the note of conscious victory
through Jesus Christ. The nearer our life is
tuned to that note of conscious victory, the
greater the victory that will be evidenced in
our life.

Beloved, in the Christian life, in the heart

of God, there is an ultimate note. It is that note which is so fine and sweet and true and pure and good that it causes all our nature to respond to it, and rejoices the soul with a joy unspeakable.

All down through the ages some have touched God and heard that ultimate note. I believe that as David sat on the mountainside as a boy, caring for his father's sheep, God by the Spirit taught him the power and blessing of that ultimate note. I believe at times that his soul ascended unto God so that many of the Psalms of David are the real soul note of that blessed expression of heavenly music and heaven consciousness which came into the soul of the shepherd boy.

Lord, make of my life a high note, a new song of praise and rejoicing in You. Amen.

Day 2

A Strong Man's Gospel

Let the weak say, I am strong.
—JOEL 3:10

E SEE THE NOTE that was in the soul of Paul, and which characterized his message, when he made the splendid declaration, "For I am not ashamed of the gospel of Christ: for it is the power of God unto salvation to every one that believeth; to the Jew first, and also to the Greek" (Rom. 1:16).

This bold note touched the souls of men and rang down through the centuries. This bold note rings in your heart and mine today. Christianity never was designed by God to make a lot of weaklings. It was designed to bring forth a race of men who were bold and strong and pure and good.

The greatest, strongest, and the noblest is always the humblest. The beautiful thing in the gospel is that it eliminates from the life of man that which is of himself and is natural and fleshly and earthly. It brings forth the beauteous things within the soul of man—the unselfishness, the life of purity, the peace, the strength, and the power of the Son of God.

How beautiful it is to have the privilege of looking into the face of one whose nature has been thus refined by the Spirit of the living God within. How beautiful it is when we look into the soul of one who has been purged by the blood of Christ until the very characteristics of the life and attitudes of the mind of Christ are manifest.

Christianity is a strong man's gospel. Christianity, by the grace of God, is calculated to take the weak, fallen, erring, suffering, dying, and apply the grace and power of God, through the soul of man, to the need of the individual.

> *Lord, transform my weakness into strength and my timidity into boldness. Amen.*

Day 3

Divine Mastery Through Christ

I am he that liveth, and was dead; and,
behold, I am alive for evermore, Amen;
and have the keys of hell and of death.
— REVELATION 1:18

WHEN THE LORD Jesus Christ is born indeed in our souls, and we yield ourselves to God by the grace and power of the Son of God, our natures possess that Spirit which is in Christ (Rom. 8:11). Then we begin to realize the spirit of mastery that Jesus possessed. That is the reason I do not spend much time talking about the devil. The Lord took care of him, bless God! Jesus has the keys of hell and of death, and He has mastered the enemy once and for all.

If you and I had as much faith to believe that the enemy is mastered as we have to believe that the Lord Jesus Christ is our Savior, we would have mighty little trouble with the devil or his power while we walk through this old world. Jesus said, "Behold, I give unto you power to tread on serpents and scorpions, and over all the power of the enemy: and nothing shall by any means hurt you" (Luke 10:19).

It is not worthwhile talking about an enemy after he is wiped out. It is a hard thing for the Christian mind to conceive that the power of evil is really a vanquished power.

Beloved, you and I have bowed our heads before a vanquished enemy. We have failed through lack of faith to comprehend that Christ is the Master. He who dares by the grace of God to look into the face of the Lord Jesus Christ knows within his own soul the divine mastery that the Christ of God is exercising now.

> *Lord, help me to see myself as You see me: more than a conqueror in You. Amen.*

Day 4

Sin and Sickness

*In the day that thou eatest thereof
[sinnest] thou shalt surely die.*
—GENESIS 2:17

WHENEVER WE SIN—partake of that which
is earthy—the decayed conditions of
the earth begin the death process in us. Death
ruled in our bodies from the time that sin came.

Sickness is incipient death. Death is the
result of sin (Rom. 6:23; 1 Cor. 15:56). There
is no sickness in God. There never was. There
never will be. There never can be.

There was no sickness in Adam—created a
spirit being without sin—until such time as he
became the earth—man, when by the operation of will he sank into himself and became
earthy. Therefore, sin is the parent of sickness
in that broad sense. Sickness is the result of
sin. There could have been no sickness if there
had been no sin.

Having fallen into that condition and become separated from God, humanity needed a Redeemer—Jesus Christ. Redemption was a necessity because the Word says "Ye must be born again" (John 3:7).

Not just any man could redeem us from sin and death. Only a God-man without sin could save and heal us.

The last Adam, Jesus, had no sin. As a man tempted in every aspect as we are (Heb. 4:15), he could have sinned. But Jesus triumphed over that condition of fallen human nature and did not sin. This is what makes Him a sympathetic Savior and Christ.

Lord Jesus, You are my redeemer from death, sin, and sickness. Amen.

Day 5

The Secret Is Being

Beloved, now are we the sons of God, and it doth not yet appear what we shall be: but we know that, when he shall appear, we shall be like him.

—1 JOHN 3:2

A LOW STANDARD of Christianity is responsible for all the shame and sin and wickedness in the world. Many Christians think it is all right if they only partially pattern their lives after Jesus. They imitate Him and do the things which He did—that is, they outwardly do them. They perform kind acts and attempt to be good.

But the secret of Christianity is not in *doing*. The secret is in *being*. Real Christianity is in being a possessor of the nature of Jesus Christ. In other words, it is being Christ in character, Christ in demonstration, and Christ in agency of transmission. When one gives himself to the Lord and becomes a child of God, all that he does and all that he says from that time on, should be the will, the words, and the actions of Jesus, just as absolutely and as entirely as Jesus spoke and did the will of the Father.

Jesus showed us that the only way to live this life was to commit oneself, as He did, to the will of God. He did not walk in His own ways at all, but walked in God's ways. So the one who is going to be a Christian in the best sense and let the world see Jesus in him, must walk in all the ways of Jesus by following Him. He must *be* a Christ-man or Christ-woman— a Christian, or Christ-one.

> *Jesus, I'm tired of being like others. I desire to be totally committed to being who God wills me to be—His child, a Christian. Amen.*

The Mind of Christ

For who hath known the mind of the Lord, that he may instruct him? But we have the mind of Christ.
—1 CORINTHIANS 2:16

THE MIND is the soul life, and it continues being of the earth—earthy and doing earthy things until God does something to that mind, and we seek God for a new mind. It is similar to the change which occurs in the spirit; and the mind that formerly thought evil and that had wicked conceptions becomes as the mind of Christ.

The church at large recognizes the salvation of the spirit. But they have not recognized the salvation of the mind from the power of sin, and that is why many church people will say there is no such thing as sanctification.

There are Christian bodies that believe in the power of God to sanctify the mind, even as the spirit is saved. John Wesley, in defining sanctification, says that it is: "Possessing the mind of Christ, and all the mind of Christ." An individual with all the mind of Christ cannot have a thought that is not a Christ thought, no more than a spirit fully surrendered to God could have evil within it.

> *Christ, I surrender my mind, thoughts, opinions, will, and emotions totally to You. My soul is Your territory and not mine. Amen.*

Day 7

Divine Health

Bless the Lord, O my soul, and forget not all his benefits: who forgiveth all thine iniquities; who healeth all thy diseases.
—PSALM 103:2–3

THE IMPRESSION I wish to leave is this, that an hundredfold consecration to God takes the individual forever out of the hands of all but God. This absolute consecration to God, this triune salvation, is the real secret of the successful Christian life.

When one trusts any department of his being to man, he is weak in that part of his being—not committed to God. When we trust our minds (souls) and our bodies to man, two parts are out of the hands of God, and what remains is simply our spirits in tune with heaven. It ought not to be so. The committing of the whole being to the will of God is the mind of God. Blessed be His Name.

Such a commitment of the being to God

puts one in the place where, just as God supplies health to the spirit and health to the soul, he also trusts God to supply health to his body. Divine healing is the removal by the power of God of the disease that has come upon the body, but divine health is to live day by day and hour by hour in touch with God so that the life of God flows into the body, just as the life of God flows into the mind or flows into the spirit.

The Christian, the child of God, the Christ-man or woman, who thus commits totally to God ought not to be a subject for healing. He is a subject of continuous, abiding health. And the secret of life in communion with God, the Spirit of God, is received into the physical being, into the soul, and into the spirit.

Jesus, I desire to abide in You that I might live in Your divine health. Amen.

Lift Jesus Up

And I [Jesus], if I be lifted up from the earth, will draw all men unto me.
—JOHN 12:32

MEN HAVE MYSTIFIED the gospel; they have philosophized the gospel. The gospel of Jesus is as simple as can be. As God lived in the body and operated through the man Jesus, so the man on the throne, Jesus, operates through His Body, the church, in the world. Even as Jesus Himself was the representative of God the Father, so also the church is the representative of Christ. As Jesus yielded Himself unto all righteousness, so the church should yield herself to do all the will of Christ.

"These signs shall follow them that believe" (Mark 16:17). The miraculous signs and wonders that point the world to Jesus Christ follow not just the preacher, or the elder, or the priest, but the believer. The believer shall speak in new tongues. The believer shall lay hands on the sick and they shall recover. Believers are the body of Christ in the world. The Word say that there shall be saviors in Zion (Obad. 21).

Just as Jesus, the Savior, took us, the church, lifting us up to the Father, and giving Himself to sanctify and cleanse us, so the Christian takes the world and lifts it up to Christ.

The wonderful simplicity of the gospel of Jesus is itself a marvel. The wonder is that men have not always understood the whole process of salvation. How was it that men mystified it? Why is it that we have not lived a better life? Because our eyes were dim, and we did not see, and we did not realize that God left us here in this world to demonstrate Him, even as the Father left Jesus in the world to demonstrate the Father.

Lord Jesus, I lift You up that I may lift up all men unto You. Amen.

Day 9

Power in Christ

Greater is he that is in you, than he that is in the world.

—1 JOHN 4:4

A PERSON WITH CHRIST within by the Holy Ghost is greater than any other power in the world. All other natural and evil powers are less than God. Satan is a lesser power.

Man with God in him is greater than Satan. That is the reason that God tells the believer that he shall be able to cast out devils. The Christian, therefore, is a ruler. He is in the place of dominion, the place of authority, even as Jesus was. Jesus, knowing that all power had been given unto Him, took a basin and a towel and washed His disciples' feet. His power did not exalt Him. It made Him the humblest of all men.

So the more a Christian possesses Christ's power, the more of a servant he will be. God is the great servant of the world. He is the One who continually gives to men the necessity of the hour. Through His guidance and direction of the laws of the world, He provides for all the needs of mankind. He is the great servant of the world, the greatest of all servants.

Yes, Jesus, knowing that all power had been committed to Him, commits through the Holy Ghost, by His own Spirit, all power to man.

> *Lord Jesus, grant me the strength and courage to walk in the power You have given me. Amen.*

Day 10

Shut Out Evil

Behold, I [Jesus] give unto you power to tread on serpents and scorpions, and over all the power of the enemy: and nothing shall by any means hurt you.

— LUKE 10:19

I TELL YOU, beloved, it is not necessary for people to be dominated by evil, nor by evil spirits. Instead of being dominated, Christians should exercise dominion and control other forces. Even Satan has no power over them, only as they permit him to have. Jesus taught us to close the mind, to close the heart, to close the being against all that is evil and to live with an openness to God only, so that the sunlight and glory-radiance of God shines in and shuts out everything that is dark.

Jesus said, "Take heed therefore *how* ye hear" (Luke 8:18, italics added)—not *what* you hear. One cannot help *what* he hears, but he can take heed *how* he hears. When it is something offensive to the Spirit and to the knowledge of God, shut the doors against it, and it will not touch you.

The Christian lives as God wills in the world, dominating sin, evil, and sickness. I would to God that He would be lifted up until all believers would realize their privilege in Christ Jesus.

By the Spirit within us we cast out or expel from our beings all that is not God-like. If you find within your heart a thought of sin or self-ishness, by the exercise of the Spirit of God within you, cast that thing out as unworthy of a child of God, and put it away from you. "Be ye holy; for I am holy," God says to us (1 Pet. 1:16).

> *Jesus, by Your Spirit, I cast out all unholiness, sin, and selfishness from my life as unworthy for a child of God. I shut the door of my ears to anything unholy. Amen.*

Day 11

Radiate Christ

For this purpose the Son of God was manifested, that he might destroy the works of the devil.

—1 John 3:8

EVIL IS REAL. The devil is real. He was a real angel. Pride changed his nature. God is real. The operation of God within the heart changes our nature until we are new creations in Christ Jesus, new creatures in Christ Jesus. The power of God, the Holy Ghost, is the Spirit of dominion. It makes the believer a child of God. It makes one not subject to the forces of the world, or the flesh, or the devil. These are under the Christian's feet.

Beloved, God wants us to come, to stay, and to live in that abiding place which is the Christian's estate. This is the heavenly place in Christ Jesus. This is the secret place of the most high. Bless God!

The Word of God gives us this key. It says,

"That wicked one toucheth him not" (1 John 5:18). When the Spirit of God radiated from the man Jesus, I wonder how close to Him it was possible for the evil spirit to come? Do you not see that the Spirit of God is as destructive of evil as it is creative of good? It was impossible for the evil one to come near Him, and I feel sure Satan talked to Jesus from a safe distance.

The Spirit of God radiates from the Christian's person because of the indwelling Holy Ghost and makes him impregnable to any touch or contact of evil forces. He is the subjective force himself. The Spirit of God radiates from him as long as his faith in God is active. "Resist the devil, and he will flee from you" (James 4:7).

> *Jesus, radiate through me with Your power to destroy the works of the devil around about me. Amen.*

Day 12

The Presence of Christ

*And, lo, I am with you always, even unto
the end of the world.*

—MATTHEW 28:20

SOME MAY have read the booklet by
Brother Lawrence, *Practicing the Presence of
Christ.* It speaks of a necessity in the Christian
life—His presence that is always with us.

One of the things the Christian world does
not get hold of with a strong grip is the conscious presence of Christ with us now.
Somehow there is an inclination in the
Christian spirit to feel that Jesus, when He left
the earth and returned to Glory, is not present
with us now.

I want to show you how wonderfully the
Scriptures emphasize the fact of His presence
with us now. His promise after the great
Commission to the eleven disciples was, "I am
with you always."

It would naturally seem as if a separation had been contemplated because of His return to Glory, but no such separation is contemplated on the part of Christ. Christ promises His omnipotent presence with us always. Christ is everywhere and thus omnipresent— present in the soul, present in the world, and present unto the end of the age.

Christ is the living presence of God, not only with us, but to the real Christian, He is in us as the perpetual joy, power, and glory of God. When a soul reaches to the heights of God, it will only be because of the guiding, counseling, indwelling, and infilling of the Christ.

There is a beautiful verse that expresses that so sweetly: "Closer is He than breathing, and nearer than hands and feet."

> *Draw me near, Lord, to You. I long to be in Your presence. I desire to be changed in Your presence. Amen.*

Day 13

Christ Formed in You

*Till we all come in the unity of the faith,
and . . . unto the measure of the stature
of the fullness of Christ.*
—EPHESIANS 4:13

THIS SCRIPTURE shows the ultimate purpose of Christ as Savior, of Christ as a companion, of Christ as the indwelling One. Christ's presence with us is not just as an outward companion, but an indwelling, divine force, revolutionizing our nature and making us like Him. Indeed, the final and ultimate purpose of the Christ is that the Christian shall be reproduced in His own likeness, within and without.

Paul expressed the same thing in the first chapter of Colossians, where he says, "To present you holy and unblameable and unreprovable in his sight" (v. 22). That transformation is to be an inner transformation. It is a transformation of our life, of our nature into His nature, into His likeness.

How wonderful the patience, how marvelous the power that takes possession of the soul of man and accomplishes the will of God—an absolute transformation into the beautiful holiness of the character of Jesus. Our heart staggers when we think of such a calling, when we think of such a nature, when we contemplate such a character. That is God's purpose for you and me.

In emphasizing this truth the apostle again puts it into a different form: He says, "Until Christ be formed in you" (Gal. 4:19).

That is the mission of the Lord Jesus Christ. That is the marvel He works in our lives—to transform the soul into the likeness and character of Himself, and then present us to the Father, "Holy and unblameable and unreprovable in his sight" (Col. 1:22).

Lord Jesus, by Your grace transform me into Your likeness. Amen.

Day 14

Overcome Pride

*Let this mind be in you, which was also
in Christ Jesus: Who, being in the form of
God . . . humbled himself, and became
obedient unto death.*

—PHILIPPIANS 2:5–6, 8

AT HIS last supper with the disciples,
knowing that all power had been given
unto Him, Jesus took a towel and a basin and
proceeded to wash the disciples' feet. When
He had finished He said, "Know ye what I
have done to you?" (John 13:12). In explanation He said, "If I then, your Lord and Master,
have washed your feet; ye also ought to wash
one another's feet" (John 13:14).

When we examine the human heart and
endeavor to discover what it is that retards our
progress, I believe we will find that pride in the
human soul is perhaps the greatest difficulty we
have to overcome. Jesus taught us a wonderful
humility, taking the place of a servant. We are
enjoined to thus treat and love one another.

His presence with us, His presence in us must produce in our hearts the same conditions that were in His own. It must bring into our life the same humility that was in Him. It is one of the secrets of entrance into the grace of God.

Lord Jesus, teach me to be a servant even as You served. Amen.

Day 15

A Life of Holy Triumph

*Nay, in all these things we are more than
conquerors through him that loved us.*
— ROMANS 8:37

ONE OF THE TRUEST things in all my life, in
my relationship with the Lord Jesus
Christ, has been to feel that He was capable of
knowing my sorrows, and yours. And, in the
truest sense, He thereby became our comrades.

In the Book of Isaiah there is a verse that
wonderfully expresses that fact. "In all their
affliction he was afflicted, and the angel of his
presence saved them: in his love and in his pity
he redeemed them; and he bare them, and car-
ried them all the days of old" (Isa. 63:9).

There is a union between the Christ and
the Christian that is so deep, so pure, so sweet,
so real, that the very conditions of the human
spirit are transmitted to His, and the conditions of the Christ's Spirit are transmitted to

ours. It is because of the continuous inflow of the Spirit of Christ in our hearts that we appreciate or realize His power and triumph. His Spirit lifts us above his surroundings and causes us to triumph anywhere and everywhere.

The Christian life is designed by God to be a life of splendid, holy triumph. That triumph is produced in us through the continuous inflow and abiding presence of the Spirit of the triumphant Christ. He brings into our nature the triumph that He enjoys. Indeed the mature Christian, having entered into that consciousness of overcoming through the Spirit of Christ, is privileged to transmit that same overcoming power and spirit to other lives, in and through the power of the Spirit of God.

> *In my life, Lord Jesus, bring triumph and victory over the enemy that I might glorify You for every holy triumph. Amen.*

Day 16

Abundant Life

The thief cometh not, but for to steal, and to kill, and to destroy: I am come that they might have life, and that they might have it more abundantly.
—JOHN 10:10

THERE IS a quickening by the Spirit of God so that one's body, soul, or mind and spirit all alike may become blessed, pervaded, and filled with the presence of God Himself. The Word of God is wonderfully clear along these lines. For instance, the Word of God asserts, "Thou wilt keep him in perfect peace, whose mind is stayed on thee" (Isa. 26:3). Why? "Because he trusteth in thee." That is the rest that a Christian knows whose mind has perfect trust in God.

The Word of God says that our hearts will rejoice, and our flesh will rest in hope (Ps. 16:9). Not our mind, but our very flesh shall hope and rest in God. God is to be a living presence, not only in the spirit of man, nor in the mind of man alone, but also in the flesh of man, so that God is known in all departments of life. We know God in our very flesh. We know God in our mind. We know God in our spirit.

The medium by which God undertakes to bless the world is through the transmission of Himself. The Spirit of God is His own substance, the substance of His being, the very nature and quality of the presence, being, and nature of God.

That is the secret of the abundant life of which Jesus spoke. The reason we have the more abundant life is because that by receiving God into our being, all the springs of our being are quickened by His living presence.

> *Fill me, Spirit of God, with Your life that I might rest in Your hope and rejoice in You. Amen.*

Day 17

Receive and Reveal God's Power

And God wrought special miracles by the hands of Paul.

—ACTS 19:11

THE HUMAN being is God's marvelous, wonderful instrument. You and I are the most marvelous and wonderful creatures in all God's creation in our capacity to receive and reveal God. Paul received so much of God into his being that when people brought handkerchiefs and aprons to him, his touch impregnated those articles with the loving Spirit of God, the living substance of God's being. The effect was that when these articles were laid upon those who were sick or possessed of devils, the Word says they were healed by God (Acts 19:12).

We have been so in the habit of putting Jesus or the apostles in a class by themselves. As a result, we have failed to recognize that

Jesus made provision for the same living Spirit of God that dwelt in His own life, and of which He was a living manifestation, to inhabit our lives, just as the Spirit inhabited the beings of Jesus or Paul.

The fact that people brought to Paul handkerchiefs and aprons, and these articles became impregnated with the Spirit, and people were healed when they touched them, is a demonstration that any material substance can become impregnated with the same living Spirit of God.

> *Lord Jesus, so fill me with Your Spirit*
> *that my life becomes impregnated*
> *with the same living Spirit that*
> *healed the sick through You. Amen.*

Day 18

The Ministry of the Spirit

Now we have received, not the spirit of the world, but the spirit which is of God; that we might know the things that are freely given to us of God.

—1 CORINTHIANS 2:12

THE MINISTRY of the Christian is the ministry of the Spirit. He not only ministers words to another, but he ministers the Spirit of God. It is the Spirit that inhabits the words, speaks to the spirit of another, and reveals Christ in and through him.

In the old days when I was in Africa, I would walk into the native meetings when I did not understand the languages, and would listen to the preacher for an hour, not understanding a word he said. But my soul was blessed by the presence of the Spirit.

Perhaps I had heard better words than his, perhaps clearer explanation of the Scriptures than he could give, but I was blessed by the presence of God.

The ministry of the Christian is the ministry of the Spirit. If the Christian cannot minister the Spirit of God, in the true sense he is not a Christian. If he has not the Spirit to minister, in the highest sense he has nothing to minister. Other men have intellectual knowledge, but the Christian is supposed to be the possessor of the Spirit.

A minister of Jesus Christ is as far removed above the realm of psychological influences as heaven is above the earth. He ministers God Himself into the very spirits, souls, and bodies of people.

> *Spirit of God, use me to minister Your life to others. Amen.*

Day 19

The Secret of Being

But as many as received him, to them gave he power to become the sons of God, even to them that believe on his name.
—JOHN 1:12

PEOPLE HAVE been mystified by the gospel and thus attempted to philosophize about Jesus, but the gospel is as simple as can be.

Just as God lived and operated through the body of the man, Jesus, so Jesus, the Man on the throne, operates in and through the Christian, and through His body, the church, in the world. Just as Jesus was the representative of God the Father, so the church is the representative of Christ.

And as Jesus yielded Himself unto all righteousness, so the church should yield herself to do all the will of God.

The secret of Christianity is in *being*. It is in being a possessor of the nature of Jesus Christ. In other words, it is being:

- Christ in character
- Christ in demonstration
- Christ in agency of transmission

When a person gives himself to the Lord and becomes a child of God, that person is a Christ-man or woman—a Christian. All that one does and says from that time forth should be the will, the words, and the doing of Jesus, just as absolutely and entirely as Jesus spoke and did the will of the Father.

Jesus, I long to become like You in every aspect. Transform my nature into Yours. Amen.

Day 20

Principles of God's Kingdom

And he opened his mouth, and taught them saying, Blessed are the poor in spirit: for theirs is the kingdom of heaven.
—MATTHEW 5:2–3

WHEN HE first established His kingdom, Jesus enunciated the principles upon which His government was to rest. The eight Beatitudes, as they are given in His official declaration in the Sermon on the Mount, were the great principles upon which His government was to be founded.

A principle is not a dogma or a doctrine. A *principle* is the underlying quality, that fundamental truth, upon which all other things are based. The principles of the kingdom of heaven are those underlying qualities upon which the whole structure of the Christian life rests. The real government of Jesus Christ will be founded and exercised upon the kingdom principles. The eight Beatitudes are the *principles* of the kingdom of heaven; the Sermon on the Mount is the *constitution;* and the commandments of Jesus are its *law* or *statutes.*

The kingdom is established in our hearts. The principles of Jesus Christ are settled in our own spirit. We become citizens of the kingdom of heaven. The aggregate citizenship of the kingdom in this present age constitutes the real church, which is His body. And throughout the Church Age, the working of the body is to demonstrate to the world the practicability and desirability of the kingdom of heaven, so that all men may desire the rule of Jesus in their lives.

> *Lord Jesus, as Head of the church, I yield to Your supreme authority in my life which is totally surrendered to You. Amen.*

Day 21

Intercession

Blessed are they that mourn: for they shall be comforted.

—Matthew 5:4

THIS FIGURE is taken from the old prophets, who, when the nation sinned, took upon themselves the responsibility of the nation. They put sackcloth on their bodies, and ashes on their heads, and in mourning and tears went down before God for days and weeks until the people turned to God. They became the intercessors between God and man.

Moses became the great intercessor. When God said to him, after the Israelites had made the golden calf, "Let me alone . . . that I may consume them: and I will make of thee a great nation" (Exod. 32:10). Moses said, "Wherefore should the Egyptians speak, and say, For mischief did he bring them out, to slay them in the mountains, and to consume them from the face of the earth?" (v. 12). God had said to Moses, "I will make of thee a great nation;" but Moses was big enough to turn aside the greatest honor that God could bestow upon a man, that of becoming the father of a race. He pleaded with God, "Oh, this people have sinned a great sin, and have made them gods of gold. Yet now, if thou wilt forgive their sin—and if not, blot me, I pray thee, out of thy book" (Exod. 32:31–32).

Blessed is the intercessor who comprehends the purposes of God, who understands his responsibility and possibility, who by God-given mourning and crying turns the people to God. With a heart yearning for sinners, an intercessor becomes a mourner before God, and takes upon himself the responsibility of fallen sinners. He goes down in tears and repentance before God, until people turn to God and mercy is shown to them.

> *Lord, I confess that I am a sinner dwelling in the midst of a sinful people. Forgive our sin and restore us with Your mercy. Amen.*

Day 22

Righteousness

Blessed are they which do hunger and thirst after righteousness: for they shall be filled.

—MATTHEW 5:6

HUNGER IS a mighty good thing. It is the greatest persuader I know. It is a marvelous mover. Nations have learned that you can do almost anything with a populace until they get hungry But when they get hungry you want to watch out. There is a certain spirit of desperation that accompanies hunger.

I wish we all had such desperate spiritual hunger. I wish to God we were desperately hungry for God. Wouldn't it be glorious? It would be a strange thing if we were all desperately hungry for God, but only one or two individuals got filled in a service. If everyone in a service was desperately hungry for God, how much more the whole assembly would experience the filling of the Holy Spirit.

"Blessed are they which do hunger and thirst after righteousness." *Righteousness* is "the rightness of God"—the rightness of God in your spirit, the rightness of God in your soul, the rightness of God in your body, and the rightness of God in your affairs, home, business, and in every aspect of your life.

God is an all-round God. His power operates from every side. There is a radiation of glory from His person. It is the radiant glory of the indwelling God, radiating out through the personality. There is nothing more wonderful than the indwelling of God in the human life. The most supreme marvel that God ever performed was when He took possession of those who are hungry for righteousness and filled them!

> *Lord, I am desperately hungry for Your righteousness. Fill me. Saturate me. Overflow me with Your righteousness. Amen.*

Day 23

Even Unto Death

Take, eat: this is my body, which is broken for you.

—1 CORINTHIANS 11:24

WE COME to the last night of the Lord's life. He is with His disciples in the upper room. Here comes the final act, the consummation of all His life. There is a phase of this act I know the Lord has not made clear to many.

They sat around the table after they had eaten their supper. Jesus took bread and brake it, and instructed them to take and eat. What did He mean? Since He was there in the flesh, what was the significance of the breaking of bread?

By that act the Lord Jesus Christ pledged Himself before God, before the holy angels, and before men, that He would not stop short of dying for the world. There was no limit. He was faithful even unto death.

Just as He had been faithful in life, and had lived each day conscious of everything in life around him, so now He would fix His entire being on the cross. He is going to be faithful *even unto death.*

The real purpose of becoming a Christian is not to save yourself from hell, or to be saved to go to heaven. It is to become a child of God, with the character of Jesus Christ to stand before men, pledged unto the uttermost, *even unto death,* by refusing to sin, refusing to bow your head in shame, preferring to die rather than to dishonor the Son of God.

If the character of Jesus Christ has entered into you and into me, then it has made us like Him in purpose. It has made us like Him in fact. Bless God! His Spirit is imparted to us. Bless God for that same unquenchable fidelity that characterized the Son of God.

> *Jesus, for me to live or die for You is gain. Amen.*

Day 24

The Cross of Christ

But God forbid that I should glory, save in the cross of our Lord Jesus Christ, by whom the world is crucified unto me, and I unto the world.

—GALATIANS 6:14

Men have said that the cross of Christ was not a heroic thing, but I want to tell you that the cross of Jesus Christ has put more heroism in the souls of men than any other event in human history. Men have lived, rejoiced, and died believing in the living God, in the Christ of God whose blood cleansed their hearts from sin, and who have realized the real high spirit of His holy sacrifice, bless God.

They manifested to mankind that same measure of sacrifice, and endured all that human beings could endure. When endurance was no longer possible, they passed on to be with God, leaving the world blessed through the evidence of a consecration deep and true and pure and good, like the Son of God Himself.

> *Jesus, I lay at the foot of Your cross all my sin and weakness. Cleanse me with Your blood and empower me to take up my cross and follow You whatever the cost. Amen.*

Day 25

The Higher Life

And hath raised us up together, and made us sit together in heavenly places in Christ Jesus.

—EPHESIANS 2:6

ELOVED, that is the difficulty with us all. We have come down out of the heavenlies into the natural, and we are trying to live a heavenly life in the natural state, overburdened by the weights and cares of the flesh and life all about us. Bless God, there is deliverance. There is victory. There is a place in God where the flesh no longer becomes a bondage. Where, by the grace of God, every sensuous state of the human nature is brought into subjection to the living God, where Christ reigns in and glorifies the very activities of a man's nature, making him sweet and pure and clean and good and true.

I call you today, beloved, by the grace of God, to that higher life, to that holy walk, to that heavenly atmosphere, to that life in God where the grace and Spirit and power of God permeate your whole being. Where not only your whole being is in subjection, but Gods Spirit flows from your nature as a holy stream of heavenly life to bless other souls everywhere by the grace of God.

> *Be Thou my strength, Lord Jesus, that Your higher life may permeate my entire being so that I may bless others in Your grace. Amen.*

Day 26

Be an Overcomer

To him that overcometh will I give to eat
of the tree of life, which is in the midst of
the paradise of God.

—REVELATION 2:7

I HAVE BEEN a student all my life. Not just a student of letters, but of the things of the soul. God helped me by His grace to take note of and analyze the conditions of my own soul. I noted that when that high consciousness of heavenly dominion rested upon my life, there was one thing that stood uppermost in all my consciousness. That was the vision of the triumphant Christ, the Son of God, as pictured by John in the first chapter of Revelation, where He stands forth in the mighty dignity of an overcomer. Jesus declares, "I am he that liveth, and was dead; and, behold, I am alive for evermore, Amen; and have the keys of hell and of death" (Rev. 1:18).

Beloved, I want to tell you that the soul joined to Christ, and who exercises the power of God, ascends into that high consciousness of heavenly dominion as is in the heart of Jesus Christ today, for He is the overcomer, the only overcomer. But yet, when my soul is joined to His soul, when His Spirit flows like a heavenly stream through my spirit, when my whole nature is infilled and inspired by the life from God, I too, being joined with Him, become an overcomer in deed and in truth. Glory be to God.

By faith, I declare upon the Word that I am an overcomer in Christ, and desire His overcoming life to flow through me. Amen.

Unlimited Life

*Till we all come in the unity of the faith,
and of the knowledge of the Son of God,
unto a perfect man, unto the measure of
the stature of the fullness of Christ.*

—EPHESIANS 4:13

CHRISTIANITY IS not a thing to be apologized for. Christianity is the living, conscious life and power of the living God, transmitted into the nature of man until our nature is transformed by the living touch, and our very spirit, soul, and being is energized and filled by His life.

That startles some people. But the ultimate of the gospel of Jesus Christ and the ultimate of the redemption of the Son of God is to reproduce and make every man—bound by sin, held by sensuousness, and enslaved by the flesh—like Himself in deed and in truth, sons of God. Not sons of God on a lower order, but sons of God as Jesus is.

Christians do not live a limited life, but an

unlimited life. The idea of Christ, the idea of God was that every man, through Jesus Christ, through being joined to Him by the Holy Spirit, should be transformed into Christ's perfect image. Christ within and Christ without. Christ in your spirit, Christ in your soul, and Christ in your body.

Not only living His life in you, but performing His works by the grace of God. That is the gospel of the Son of God.

> *Lord Jesus, my desire is to be more like You, with You living Your life and doing Your work in me. Amen.*

Day 28

Unselfishness

If any man will come after me, let him deny himself, and take up his cross, and follow me.

—MATTHEW 16:24

SOME BECOME Christians in order to save themselves from hell. Others go a step further, and you can note the ascending consciousness. They say, "No, saving yourself from hell and punishment is not the ideal of the gospel. The ideal is to get saved so as to go to heaven." And so men were saved in order to get to heaven when they died. I have always had a feeling in my soul of wanting to weep when I hear men pleading with others to become Christians so they will go up to heaven when they die. My God, is there no appeal outside of something absolutely selfish?

Beloved, don't you see that Christianity was unselfishness. It had no consideration for the selfish individual. The ideal held up above everything else in the world, and the only ideal worthy of a Christian was that we in Christ might demonstrate to humanity one holy, high, beauteous thing, of which the world was deficient, and that was a knowledge of God. So Jesus said, "It becometh us to fulfill all righteousness" (see Matt. 3:15), and He wrote it on the souls of men, branded it on their consciences, and stamped it on their hearts until the world began to realize the unselfish ideal that was in the soul of Jesus.

To fulfill all righteousness is like Christ Himself, a demonstrator of the righteousness of the living God. That is Christianity, and that only is Christianity, for that was the consecration of the Christ Himself.

Jesus, You are my unselfish example for living life. Amen.

Day 29

By Their Fruits

Wherefore by their fruits ye shall know them.

—Matthew 7:20

THE TEST of the Spirit, and the only test of the Spirit that Jesus ever gave, is the ultimate and final test. He said, "By their fruits ye shall know them" (Matt. 7:20). That is the absolute and final test. "Do men gather grapes of thorns, or figs of thistles?" (Matt. 7:16).

So I say to you, if you want to test whether this present outpouring of the Spirit of God is the real thing, the real pure baptism of the Holy Ghost or not, test it by the fruits that it produces. If, as we believe, it is producing in the world a consciousness of God so high, so pure, so acceptable, so true, so good, so like Christ, then it is the Holy Ghost Himself. No other test is of any value whatever.

I want to tell you, Beloved, that the ultimate

test of the value of a thing that you have in your heart is the common test that Jesus gave, "By their fruits ye shall know them."

Jesus, produce in my life Your fruit that others may know You through me. Amen.

What Is Sin?

*All these evil things come from within,
and defile the man.*

—MARK 7:23

MEN TELL US in these days that sin is what you think it is. Well, it is not. Sin is what God thinks it is. You may think according to your own conscience, God thinks according to His. God thinks in accordance with the heavenly purity of His own nature. Man thinks in accordance with the degree of purity that his soul realizes. But the ultimate note is in God.

When men rise up in their souls' aspirations to the place of God's thought, then the character of Jesus Christ will be evident in their lives. The sweetness of His nature, the holiness of His character, and the beauty of the crowning glory that not only overshadowed Him, but that also radiated from Him will shine through us. And the genuine life of the real Christian is the inner life, the life of the soul.

"Out of the heart proceed . . . all these evil things" (Mark 7:21–23). These are the things common to the flesh of man. Out of the soul of man, likewise, proceeds by the same common law, the beauty, virtue, peace, power, and truth of Jesus, as the soul knows it.

So he whose soul is joined to Christ may now, today, this hour, shed forth as a benediction upon the world the glory and blessing and peace and power of God, even as Jesus shed it forth to all men to the praise of God.

Shine out of my heart, Lord Jesus. Amen.

Redemption

*Forasmuch as ye know that ye were not
redeemed with corruptible things . . . but
with the precious blood of Christ, as of a
lamb without blemish and without spot.*
— 1 PETER 1:18–19

THE MIND of the world is fixed on the
Redeemer. The Old Testament Scriptures, looking forward to Christ, are particularly
prolific in their description of His life, His
sorrows, His sufferings, His death, and His
sacrifice. All these were qualities of the
Redeemer.

What redemption means is best seen by following the chain of Christ's life from the
Crucifixion until now. If you want to understand the Redeemer, see Him before the cross
comes into view.

The great majority of the Christian world is
still weeping at the foot of the cross. The
consciousness of man is fixed on the Christ
who died, not on the Christ who lives. They

are looking back to the Redeemer who was, not the Redeemer who is.

On this side of the cross we see all the marvel of the opposite of what we see in the Christ on the other side of the cross. On the other side of the cross we see a man of sorrows, acquainted with grief, bearing our sicknesses, and carrying our sorrows.

On this side of the cross is the victory of His resurrection, the marvel of all victories— the victory over death by which He took death captive. A living man, Himself, He came forth the Conqueror of death itself, having put all things under His feet. What an ascent into triumph! What a change in His consciousness! What a distinction between the Redeemer and the redeemed!

> *O Redeemer, I thank You for the cross and all You did to lift me from the poverty of sin to the glorious victory! Amen.*

Day 32

Living Triumph

But now is Christ risen from the dead, and become the first fruits of them that slept.

—1 CORINTHIANS 15:20

I WANT YOU to see beyond the crucified Savior to the risen Christ. The vision of the Christ *who* is empowers you to ascend in consciousness and union with the overcoming Son of God. You are not bowed and bound with the humiliated Savior, but joined in holy glory and triumphant with the Son of God, who obtained the victory, and revealed it, and distributes its power and glory to the souls of men.

"As he is, [not as He was] so are we in this world" (1 John 4:17). Not in the life to come. The glory is not for the life that is coming, but for the life that is now. Resurrection victory is not for the future. It is for the *now*. It is not for the good days by and by. It is for the now. Not for heaven to come, but for heaven on earth now.

Sin, sickness, death are under His feet. Hell itself is taken captive and is obedient to His word. Every enemy of mankind throttled, bound, chained by the Son of God. Mankind joined with Him by the Holy Ghost in living triumph.

When I receive of the Spirit of Jesus Christ, of the Christ who is, I receive the spirit of victory and power and might and dominion, of grace, of love, of power, and of all the blessed estate of which Jesus Himself is now the conscious Master. All these things He gives to the Christian through imparting to him the Holy Ghost.

Risen Lord, empower me to capture the vision of Your resurrection that I may live in victory and power. Amen.

Beyond the Cross

*Looking unto Jesus the author and fin-
isher of our faith; who for the joy that
was set before him endured the cross.*
—HEBREWS 12:2

SHOULD I CARRY your soul into the place
of victory in God, I must carry it into the
consciousness of Christ's overcoming life. All
His healing virtue, saving grace, transforming
spirit, with all the angelic communion and the
glorious triumph of Jesus Christ is birthed in
your consciousness from the resurrection and
revealed in this revelation: "As He is, so are we
in this world" (1 John 4:17).

Jesus in His earthly life anticipated His
kingdom and triumph. He exhibited in this
world, in a measure, that victory and triumph
that His soul knew and envisioned. But when
the cross came He actually entered into the
life that His soul formerly envisioned and
knew through the Word of God and the

consciousness of God within His heart.

His ministry in the Spirit is a ministry in the all power, all consciousness, all knowledge, all grace, all victory, and all salvation of God.

I pray that your soul is lifted in the Spirit of God into that glow and glory of His triumphant life. Do you know that it is only as your mind settles back into the humiliation and the suffering of the cross without the resurrection, and into the weakness, fear, and doubting of the dispensation that is past, that you grow weak and sickly, and surrender to sin? But as your soul looks forward, and possesses in the present the glorious victory that Jesus acquired, exhibits, and enjoys, pray to rise out of your sorrows and sins into that glorious triumph of the children of God.

> *Jesus, birth in me the vision and power of Your resurrection that I might live in victory. Amen.*

The Chief End of Man

But God, who is rich in mercy, for his great love wherewith he loved us, even when we were dead in sins, hath quickened us together with Christ.

—EPHESIANS 2:4–5

WHY DID GOD create man? The chief end of man is to glorify God and enjoy Him forever.

God's purpose in the creation of mankind was to develop an association on His own plane. Otherwise God would have been living eternally with baby believers or immature, underdeveloped Christians. He would have been compelled forever to associate with those who were not able to understand or comprehend His nature and character, or the marvel of His being, or the wonder of His power.

The wonder of the redemption of Jesus Christ is revealed in the matchlessness of God's purpose to transform man into His very nature, image, and fullness. "And have put on the new man, which is renewed in knowledge after the image of him that created him" (Col. 3:10).

Thereby men as sons of God become the associates of Almighty God, on His own plane of life and understanding.

When my soul saw the vision of God Almighty's marvelous purpose, I felt like falling on my face afresh and crying out, "Worthy is the Lamb that was slain!" For "as He is, so are we in this world." All the glory and power that Jesus knows at the throne of God, all the wonders of His overcoming grace, all the marvel of the greatness of His power, is yours and mine to receive through faith in the Son of God. All this we can expect through the faith of the Son of God.

> *Thank You, Lord, for renewing me in Your image. Amen.*

Day 35

Dominion

Thou madest him to have dominion over the works of thy hands; thou hast put all things under his feet.

—Psalm 8:6

UNIVERSALLY, MAN has believed that somewhere God was going to give dominion back to him. He believed that dominion would come through his union with God, if that union could be affected. It was the universal knowledge, universal need, and the universal cry of man for union with deity that caused the incarnation.

Let me come a step closer. On the ground of what Jesus Christ did, the substitutionary sacrifice, God is able to redeem us from our sins. He is able to impart to us His very nature. He is able to give us eternal life and take us into His own family so that we can call Him "Father," not by adoption only, but by an actual birth of our spirit. So we come into actual relationship and union with God, and the age-old cry of universal man has been fulfilled.

This thing I am teaching you about our union with God is not known in the great body of Christians. All they have experienced is forgiveness of sin. There is no actual union with God. They do not know that the new birth is a real incarnation. They do not know that they become the sons and daughters of God Almighty. Jesus was the firstfruits of this, and we follow through His sacrifice.

That incarnation that God has given through the new birth has bestowed upon us the lost authority of the Garden of Eden.

Lord, in You I have dominion over sickness, bondage, and sin. Amen.

Day 36

Christ Our Righteousness

But of him are ye in Christ Jesus, who of God is made unto us wisdom, and righteousness, and sanctification, and redemption.

—1 CORINTHIANS 1:30

HERE IS OUR position through Jesus Christ: He has become our righteousness. We have become His very sons and daughters. Yet you sing weakness, talk weakness, pray weakness, and sing unbelief. You are like that good old woman. She said, "I do love that doctrine of falling from grace, and I practice it all the time." Another man said, "Brother, I believe in the dual nature. I believe that when I would do good, evil is always present with me, and I thank God that evil is always there."

You live it and you believe it, and God cannot do anything with you. You magnify failure, and you deify failure until, to the majority of you, the devil is bigger than God.

If you look in the Book of Genesis, you will

see the size of God. It is full-size photograph. And when you see Jesus Christ rising from the dead, you have seen the God-sized photograph of redemption. We reign as kings in the realm of life.

Jesus has taken Satan's badge of dominion and authority that Adam had given him in the Garden of Eden. Every person that accepts Jesus Christ is identified with Him.

Jesus did it for you. He died as your substitute and representative and became your righteousness. When He put His heel on Satan's neck, He did it for you. And to you who believe Satan is conquered and defeated, Satan can holler and bellow as much as he wants to, but you withstand him in the faith of Jesus Christ.

> *Jesus, in You the enemy has been defeated for me, and You are my righteousness and authority to reign with dominion and power. Amen.*

Day 37

Repent of Denying God's Power

For I am not ashamed of the gospel of Christ: for it is the power of God unto salvation to every one that believeth; to the Jew first, and also to the Greek.

—ROMANS 1:16

IN EVERY LAND, among every people, throughout all history, there have been occasions when a demonstration of the power of God was just as necessary to the world as it was in the days of Elijah (1 Kings 18:17–40). It is necessary now.

The people in Elijahs day had turned away from God. They had forgotten that there was a God in Israel. They were trusting in other gods, just as people are today. If I were to call you *heathen,* I suppose most people would be offended.

There are no people with more gods than the average American. Men are bowing down to the god of medicine. Men are bowing down to the god of popularity. Men are as afraid of the opinion of their neighbors as any heathen ever was in any time in the world. There is practically no Christian who has the stamina to stand forth and declare his absolute convictions concerning Jesus Christ, *the Son of God.* Much less have men the necessary stamina to declare their convictions as to Jesus Christ, *the Savior of mankind.*

That is the reason that the modern church has lost her touch with God and has gone into a sleep unto death, a sleep that can only end in spiritual death and the disintegration of the church as she stands. The only power that will revive the church in this world is that which she will receive when she throws her heart open to God as the people of Israel did and says, "Lord God, we have sinned." The sin she needs to repent of is not the committing of a lot of little acts which men call sin. These are the outgrowth of what is in the heart. The thing that mankind needs to repent of is this: That they have denied the power of God.

> *Lord, we repent of denying the power*
> *of the Gospel of Jesus Christ. Amen.*

Day 38

A Consuming Fire

For our God is a consuming fire.
—HEBREWS 12:29

GOD'S CALL to Christian churches today is to come forth from their hiding place, just as Elijah came forth (2 Kings 18), declare the ground on which you meet the enemies of God, and meet them in the Name of Jesus Christ.

The time has come when the Christian church must give a new demonstration to the world. If metaphysicians, through the operation of natural laws, can produce a certain character and degree of healing, then it is up to the church of Jesus Christ and the ministers of the Son of God to demonstrate that there is a power in the blood of Jesus Christ to save and heal people unto the uttermost—not half-healed people, or half the people healed—but all I pray and believe that God's time has come for God's challenge to be fulfilled: let the fire fall.

There was no bluffing with the Israelite prophets of old. When the people came, they laid their sacrifices on the altar, and they did not put artificial fire under it. Instead, Elijah bowed down before God. He lifted his heart to heaven, and when the fire came down and consumed the sacrifice, that was the evidence that the sacrifice was accepted.

The time has come when God wants the fire to fall; and if you, my beloved brother and sister, will pay God's price and make Christ's consecration of yourself to God, we will see God's fire fall. And it will not be destructive either, except that sin, selfishness and sickness will wither under that fire, while purity, life, holiness, and character will stand forth purified and refined by the glory and power of God's fire that comes from heaven—His fire that destroys sin and creates righteousness.

Lord, let Your fire fall upon my life, that Your righteousness might shine forth. Amen.

Believe When You Pray

*When ye pray, believe that ye receive
them, and ye shall have them.*
—MARK 11:24

GOD IS NOT the God of the dead. He is the
God of the living. The desire in my soul is
that in this nation God Almighty may raise up
an altar unto the living God, not unto a dead
God. Humanity needs an altar to the living
God, to the God that hears prayer, to the God
that answers prayer, and to the God that
answers by fire.

God is saying, "If there is a Christian, let
him pray. If there is a God, let Him answer."

In emphasizing this, the Lord Jesus Christ
says to the world, "When ye pray, believe that
ye receive them, and ye shall have them"
(Mark 11:24). That is what is the matter. Your
blank check is not worth ten cents in your
hands. Why? Because you do not believe God.

Fill in your check, believe God, and it will come to pass.

The call of Elijah (2 Kings 18) is the call of the present hour. If the Christ is the Christ, get your answers from Him. If Jesus is the Son of God, with power on the earth to forgive sins, then as Jesus put it, "Arise, and take up thy bed, and walk . . . that ye may know that the Son of man hath power on earth to forgive sins" (Mark 2:10).

Jesus Christ was reasonable enough to meet man's reasonings and inquiries. And the minister of God who is afraid to walk out and believe his God, and trust his God for results is no Christian at all.

What does Christianity mean to the world? Is it a hope for the glory land away off in the future? Is that Christianity? Is it a hope that you are not going to fry in hell? No! Christianity is the demonstration of the righteousness of God to the world.

Lord, fill me with faith to pray with confidence in Your powerful answer. Amen.

Day 40

Early Christians

*And with great power gave the apostles
witness of the resurrection of the Lord
Jesus: and great grace was upon them all.*
—ACTS 4:33

EVERY STUDENT of the primitive church
discerns at once a distinction between
the soul of the early Christians and the soul of
the modern Christians. It lies in the spirit of
Christ's dominion.

The Holy Spirit came into the first-century
Christian soul to elevate his consciousness in
Christ, to make him a master. He smote sin,
and it disappeared. He cast out devils
(demons); a divine flash from his nature over-
powered and cast out the demon. He laid his
hands on the sick, and the mighty Spirit of
Jesus Christ flamed into the body, and the disease was annihilated. He was commanded to
rebuke the devil, and the devil would flee
from him. The early Christian was a reigning

sovereign, not shrinking in fear, but over-coming by faith.

It is this spirit of dominion when restored to the church of Christ, that will bring again glorious triumph to the church throughout the world.

Taking dominion, God's Spirit will lift the church into the place, where, instead of being the obedient servant of the world, the flesh, the devil, she will become the divine instrument of salvation in healing the sick, casting out of devils (demons), and carrying out of the whole program of Jesus' ministry as the early church did.

> *Fill me, Lord Jesus, with the same power of dominion over creation that permeated the early Christians. Amen.*

The Soul Cry of Prayer

*For they had sworn with all their heart,
and sought him [God] with their whole
desire, and he was found of them.*
—2 CHRONICLES 15:15

E ARE SOMETIMES inclined to think of God as mechanical; as though God set a date for this event or that to occur. But my opinion is that one of the works of the Holy Ghost is that of preparer. He comes and *prepares* the heart of His people in advance by putting a strange hunger for that event that has been promised by God until it comes to pass.

The more I study history and prophecy, the more I am convinced that when Jesus Christ was born into the world, He was born in answer to a tremendous heart cry on the part of the world.

Daniel says that he was convinced by the study of the books of prophecy, especially that of Jeremiah, that the time had come when they ought to be delivered from their captivity in Babylon. The seventy years were fulfilled, but there was no deliverance. So he diligently set his face to pray it into being (Dan. 9).

Here is what I want you to get: If it was going to come to pass mechanically on a certain date, there would not have been any necessity for Daniel to get that awful hunger in his soul, so causing him to fast and pray, that the deliverance might come.

God's purposes come to pass when your heart and mine get the real God-cry and the real God-prayer comes into our spirit, and the real God-yearning gets hold of our nature. Something is going to happen then.

> *Lord, my soul cry is for Your will to come to pass in my life. Amen.*

Day 42

Spiritual Hunger

As the hart panteth after the water brooks,
so panteth my soul after thee, O God.
—PSALM 42:1

I LIVED IN a family where for thirty-two years we were never without an invalid in the home. Before I was twenty-four years of age we had buried four brothers and four sisters, and four other members of the family were dying, hopeless, helpless invalids. I set up my own home, married a beautiful woman. Our first son was born. It was only a short time until I saw that same devilish train of sickness that had followed my father's family had come into mine. My wife became an invalid, my son was a sickly child. Out of it all one thing developed in my nature, *a cry for deliverance.*

I did not know any more about the subject of healing than a heathen, notwithstanding I was a Methodist evangelist. But my heart was crying for deliverance; my soul had come to the place where I had vomited up dependence on man. My father had spent a fortune on the family, to no avail, as if there were no stoppage to the train of hell. And let me tell you, there is no human stoppage, because the thing is settled deep in the nature of man, too deep for any material remedy to get at it.

It takes the Almighty God, the Holy Spirit, and the Lord Jesus Christ to get down into the depth of man's nature and find the real difficulty that is there and destroy it.

> *I hunger for Your presence and healing, Lord Jesus. Nothing but You can satisfy my spiritual hunger. Amen.*

Day 43

Praying With Conviction

The effectual, fervent prayer of a right-eous man availeth much.

—James 5:15

ONE DAY DON Von Vuuren received a letter from friends in Johannesburg telling of the coming of what they spoke of as "the American brethren," and of the wonderful things that were taking place. Of how So-and-so, a terrible drunkard, had been converted. Of how his niece who had been an invalid in a wheelchair for five years had been healed of God, and how one of his other relatives had been baptized in the Holy Ghost and was speaking in tongues. And all the marvels a vigorous work for God produces.

Don Von Vuuren took the letter and crawled under an African thorn tree. He spread the letter out before God, and began to discuss it with the Lord. He said, "God in heaven, if You could come to Mr. So-and-so, a drunkard, and deliver him from his sin and save his soul and put the joy of God in him; if You could come to this niece of mine, save her soul and heal her body and send her out to be a blessing instead of a weight and burden upon her friends; and if You could come to So-and-so and he was baptized in the Holy Ghost and spoke in tongues, then Lord, You can do something for me too." So he knelt down, put his face to the ground, and cried to God.

And God came down into his life. In ten minutes he took all the breath he wanted; the pain was gone, his tuberculosis had disappeared, he was a whole man.

Lord, so empower my prayers that they are not only effective for change in my life but also for change in the lives of others. Amen.

Seek With Faith and Prayer

*And all things, whatsoever ye shall ask in
prayer, believing, ye shall receive.*
—MATTHEW 21:22

WILLIAM SEYMOUR told me, "Brother,
before I met Parham, such a hunger to
have more of God was in my heart that I
prayed for five hours a day for two-and-a-half
years. I got to Los Angeles, and when I got
there the hunger was not less but more. I
prayed, 'God, what can I do?' And the Spirit
said, 'pray more.' 'But Lord, I am praying five
hours a day now.' I increased my hours of
prayer to seven, and prayed on for a year-and-
a-half more. I prayed, 'God, give me what
Parham preached, the real Holy Ghost and
fire with tongues and love and power of God
like the apostles had.'"

There are better things to be had in spiritual life but they must be sought out with

faith and prayer. I want to tell you God Almighty had put such a hunger into Seymour's heart that when the fire of God came it glorified him.

I wonder what we are hungering for? Have we a real divine hunger, something our soul is asking for? If we have, God will answer, God will answer. By every law of the Spirit that men know, the answer is due to come. It will come! Bless God, it will come. It will come in more ways than we ever dreamed.

Lord, teach me to pray in faith that I might receive all that You have for me. Amen.

Christ Living in Us

*I am crucified with Christ: nevertheless I
live; yet not I, but Christ liveth in me.*
—GALATIANS 2:20

THAT IS the text, "Christ liveth in me."
That is the revelation of this age. That is
the discovery of the moment. That is the revolutionizing power of God in the earth. It is
the factor that is changing the spirit of religion
in the world and the character of Christian
faith. It is divine vitalization. The world is
awakening to that marvelous truth, that
Christ is not in the heavens only, nor in the
atmosphere only, but Christ is in you.

The world lived in darkness for thousands
of years. There was just as much electricity in
the world then as now. It is not that electricity
has just come into being. It was always here.
But men have discovered how to utilize it and
bless themselves with it.

Christ's indwelling in the human heart is the mystery of mysteries. Paul gave it to the Gentiles as the supreme mystery of all the revelation of God and the finality of all wonder he knew. "Christ in you."

Christ has a purpose in you. Christ's purpose in you is to reveal Himself to you, through you and in you. We repeat over and over that familiar phrase, "The church, which is his body" (Eph. 1:22–23), but if we realized the truth and power of it, this world would be a different place.

Christ, live in and through me. Amen.

Day 46

The Marks of the Lord Jesus

I bear in my body the marks of the Lord Jesus.

—GALATIANS 6:17

YOU NOTICE among the most devout Christians how continuously their thought is limited to that place where they can be exercised or moved by God. But God's best is more than that.

While I was in Chicago, I met a couple of old friends who invited me to dinner. While at dinner the lady, who is a very frank woman, said: "Mr. Lake, I have known you so long and have had such close fellowship with you for so many years, that I am able to speak very frankly."

I said, "Yes, absolutely."

"Well," she said, "there is something I miss about you. For lack of words I am going to put it in Paul's words, 'I bear in my body the marks of the Lord Jesus' (Gal. 6:17). You do not seem to have the marks of Jesus."

I said, "That depends whether or not it is the marks of mannerisms. If you are expecting that the personality that God gave me is going to be changed so that I am going to be another fellow and not myself, then you will miss it. If that is the kind of marks you are looking for you will not find them.

"But if you are expecting to observe a man's flesh and blood and bones and spirit and mind indwelt by God, then you will find them—not a machine, not an automaton, or an imitation, but a clear mind and a pure heart, a son of God in nature and essence."

All God's effort with the world is to bring out the real man in the image of Christ, that real man with the knowledge of God. That real man, reconstructed until his very substance is the substance of God.

I desire to bear Your marks, Lord Jesus, in my body. Manifest Your vision and touch in me. Amen.

Day 47

The Greatest of These Is Love

*Now abideth faith, hope, charity, these
three; but the greatest of these is charity
[love].*

—1 Corinthians 13:13

THERE IS ONE great thing that the world is
needing more than anything else, and I
am convinced of it every day I live. Humanity
has one supreme need, and that is the love of
God. The hearts of men are dying for lack of
the love of God.

I have a sister in Detroit. She came over to
Milwaukee to visit us for two or three days at
the convention there. As I watched her
moving around, I thought, *I would like to take
her along and just have her love folks.* She would
not need to preach. You do not need to preach
to folks. It is not the words you say that are
going to bless them. They need something
greater. It is the thing in your soul. They have
to receive it, then their soul will open and

there will be a divine response. Give it to them, it is the love of God.

You have seen people who loved someone who would not respond. If there is any hard situation in God's earth, that is it, to passionately love someone and find no response in them.

Teach me, Lord, to love others the way
You love them. Amen.

𝔓𝔯𝔞𝔶𝔦𝔫𝔤 𝔉𝔯𝔬𝔪 𝔱𝔥𝔢 𝔥𝔢𝔞𝔯𝔱

A new heart also will I give you, and a new spirit will I put within you: and I will take away the stony heart out of your flesh, and I will give you a heart of flesh.
—EZEKIEL 36:26

THERE IS probably no more delightful thing on earth than to watch a soul praying to God, when the light of God comes on and the life of God fills the nature, and that holy affection that we seek from others finds expression in Him.

That is what the Lord is asking from you; and if you want to gratify the heart of Jesus Christ, that is the only way in all the world to do it. The invitation from Christ is not, "Give Me thine *head.*" The invitation is, "My son, give Me thine *heart.*" That is an affectionate relationship, a real love union in God.

Think of the fineness of God's purpose. He expects that same marvelous spiritual union that is brought to pass between your soul and

His own to be extended so that you embrace in that union every other soul around you.

Oh, that is what it means when it talks about being baptized in one spirit— submerged, buried, enveloped, and enveloping the one Spirit of God.

I come to You, Lord Jesus, with my whole heart surrendered to Your love so that Your heart might be formed anew within me to love others. Amen.

Day 49

Love With Your Whole Self

*Jesus said unto him, Thou shalt love the
Lord thy God with all thy heart, and
with all thy soul, and with all thy mind.
This is the first and great commandment.*
—Matthew 22:37–38

WE BOAST OF our development in God.
We speak glowingly of our spiritual
experiences, but it is only once in a while that
we find ourselves in the real love of God. The
greater part of the time we are in ourselves
rather than in Him. That evidences just one
thing—that Christ has not yet secured that
perfect control of our lives—that subjection of
our natures, that absorption of our individual-
ities, so that He is able to impregnate it and
maintain it in Himself. We recede, draw back,
close up, and imprison our Lord.

The secret of worship is that it assists men's
hearts to open. They become receptive, and
the love of God finds vent in their nature for a
little while. So they go away saying, "Didn't

we have a good time? Wasn't that a splendid service?"

I wonder if there is anything that could not be accomplished through the love of God. Paul says there is not. "Charity [love] never faileth" (1 Cor. 13:8). That is one infallible state. Try it on your wife, try it on your children, and try it on your neighbors.

> *Teach me to love with my whole heart, O Lord. Amen.*

Day 50

Let Go of Others

Be kindly affectioned one to another with brotherly love; in honor preferring one another.

—ROMANS 12:10

O NOT HOLD people. Do not bind people. Just cut them loose, and let God love them. Don't you know we hold people with such a grip when we pray for them that they miss the blessing. Why, you have such a grip on your humanity that it is exercising itself, and the spirit is being submerged. Let your soul relax, and let the Spirit of God in you find vent. There is no substitute for the love of God. "Christ in you" (Col. 1:27). Oh, you have the capacity to love. All the action of the Spirit of God has its secret there.

I stood on one occasion by a dying woman who was suffering and writhing in awful agony. I had prayed again and again with no results. But this day something happened inside me. My soul broke down, and I saw that poor soul in a new light. Before, I knew it I reached out and gathered her in my arms and hugged her up to my soul, not my bosom.

In a minute I knew the real thing had taken place. I laid her back down on the pillow. In five minutes she was well. God was waiting until He could get to my soul with the sense of the tenderness that was in the Son of God.

That is the reason His name is written in imperishable memory. And the name of Jesus Christ is the most revered name in earth or sea or sky. I am eager to get in that category of folks who can manifest the real love of God all the time.

> *Lord Jesus, impact my soul with a sense of Your great tenderness that I may manifest it to others. Amen.*

Day 51

Separated

I am the Lord you God, which have separated you from other people.
—LEVITICUS 20:24

THE REAL Christian is a separated man. He is separated forever unto God in all the departments of his life. So his body, soul, and spirit are forever committed to God the Father. From the time he commits himself to God, his body is as absolutely in the hands of God as his spirit or his soul. He can go to no other power for help.

A hundredfold consecration takes the individual forever out of the hands of all but God. "Ye are not your own."

Lord, separate me body, soul, and spirit solely unto You. Amen.

Day 52

The Price of Apostleship

*I have fought a good fight, I have fin-
ished my course, I have kept the faith:
Henceforth there is laid up for me a
crown of righteousness.*

—2 Timothy 4:7–8

THEY STRIPPED the Apostle Paul of his
clothing, and the executioner lashed him
with an awful scourge until, bleeding, lacer-
ated, and broken, he fell helpless, unconscious,
and insensible; then they doused him with a
bucket of salt water to keep the maggots off
and threw him into a cell to recover. That was
the price of apostleship. That was the price of
the call of God and His service. But God said,
"bear my name before the Gentiles, and kings,
and the children of Israel" (Acts 9:15). He
qualified as God's messenger.

Beloved, we have lost the character of consecration here manifested. God is trying to
restore it in our day. He has not been able to
make much progress with the average preacher

on that line. "Mrs. So-and-so said such-and-such, and I am just not going to take it." That is a preacher with another kind of call, not the heaven call, not the God call, not the death call if necessary. That is not the calling the apostle Paul had.

Jesus Christ put the spirit of martyrdom in the ministry. Jesus instituted His ministry with a pledge unto death. When He was with the disciples on the last night, He "took the cup, when he had supped, saying. . . . " (1 Cor. 11:25). Beloved, the saying was the significant thing. It was Jesus Christ's pledge to the twelve who stood with Him: "This cup is the new testament in my blood" (v. 25). Then He said, "Drink ye all of it" (Matt. 26:27).

> *Lord, strengthen me to drink of the same cup from which You drink. Amen.*

Day 53

To Die for Christ

For me to live is Christ, and to die is gain.

—PHILIPPIANS 1:21

DEAR FRIENDS, there is not an authentic history that can tell us whether any one of the disciples died a natural death. We know that at least nine of them were martyrs, possibly all. Peter died on a cross; James was beheaded; the Romans did not even wait to make a cross for Thomas—they nailed him to an olive tree. John was sentenced to be executed at Ephesus by being placed in a caldron of boiling oil. God delivered him, his executioners refused to repeat the operation, and he was banished to the Isle of Patmos.

John thought so little about it that he never tells of the incident. He says only, "I . . . was in the isle that is called Patmos, for the word of God, and for the testimony of Jesus Christ" (Rev. 1:9).

Friends, the group of missionaries that followed me went without food and clothes, and
once when one of my preachers was sun-
struck, and had wandered away, I tracked him
by the blood marks of his feet. That is the
kind of consecration that established Pentecost
in South Africa.

If I were pledging men and women to the
gospel of the Son of God, as I am endeavoring
to do now, it would not be to have a nice
church and harmonious surroundings, and a
sweet do-nothing time. I would invite them to
be ready to die. That was the spirit of early
Methodism. John Wesley established a heroic
call. He demanded every preacher to be "ready
to pray, ready to preach, ready to die." That is
always the spirit of Christianity.

> *In your hands, Lord Jesus, I put my
> life to be used by You whatever the
> cost. Amen.*

Day 54

First Desire Righteousness

Seek ye first the kingdom of God, and his righteousness; and all these things shall be added unto you.

—MATTHEW 6:33

JESUS STARTED men on the true foundation. Many simply desire health, others temporal blessings. Both are good and proper, but bless God, Jesus started the soul at the proper point, to first desire righteousness, the righteousness of God, to become a possessor of the kingdom. "Seek ye first," said Jesus, "the kingdom of God, and his righteousness."

Jesus was bringing forth and establishing in the world a new character, a character that would endure forever, a soul quality that would never fail, a faith that knew no possibility of defeat. In establishing such a character Jesus saw that the character could only be established in the depth of a man's being, in the very spirit of his being.

God has a call in His own Spirit. If we study our own spirits we will understand the nature of God. The call of the Spirit of God is the call of righteousness, the call of truth, the call of love, the call of power, the call of faith.

I met a young man on one occasion who seemed to be the most blessed man in some ways of all the men I had ever met. I observed he was surrounded by a circle of friends of men and women, the deepest and truest friendships it had ever been my privilege to know. One day I said to him, "What is the secret of this circle of friends that you possess, and the manner in which you seem to bind them to you?"

He replied, "Lake, my friendships are the result of the call of the soul. My soul has called for truth and righteousness, for holiness, for grace, for strength, for soundness of mind, for the power of God, and the call has reached this one, and this one, and this one, and brought them to me."

Lord, root all my relationship in Your righteousness. Amen.

Day 55

The Call of Righteousness

*I the Lord have called thee in righteous-
ness, and will hold thine hand, and will
keep thee, and give thee for a covenant of
the people, for a light of the Gentiles.*
—ISAIAH 42:6

IS THERE A note of despair in your heart?
Have you not obtained what your soul
covets? Have you desired to be like that sin-
less, sickless One? God will answer the call of
your heart, and you shall have your heart's
desire. But before that call becomes answer-
able, it must be the paramount call of your
being. It is when it becomes the paramount
issue of the soul that the answer comes. Jesus
knew. That is the reason He said, "Blessed are
they which do hunger and thirst after righteousness: for they shall be filled."

There is not a doubt about it. All the
barriers of your nature will go down before
the desire of the soul. All the obstacles that
ever were will disappear before the desire of

your soul. All the diseases that ever existed in your life will disappear before the desire of your soul, when that desire becomes the one great purpose and prayer of your heart.

Oh, if I had one gift, or one desire that I would bestow on you, more than all others, I would bestow upon you the hunger for God.

"Blessed are they which do hunger." Hunger is the best thing that ever came into a man's life. Hunger is hard to endure. it is the call of the nature for something that you do not possess. The thing that will satisfy the demands of the nature and the hunger of a man's soul is the call of his nature for the Spirit of life to generate the abundant love of God in him.

> *You, Lord Jesus, are my righteousness.*
> *Fill the hunger for righteousness in my*
> *life. Amen.*

The Development of the Soul

That I may know him, and the power of his resurrection, and the fellowship of his sufferings.

—PHILIPPIANS 3:10

E LIVE that our souls may grow. The development of the soul is the purpose of existence.

By His grace He is endeavoring to have us grow up in His knowledge and likeness to that stature where, as sons of God, we will comprehend something of His love, of His nature, of His power, of His purpose. Then we will be big enough to give back to God what a son should give to a great Father—the reverence, the love, the affection that comes from understanding the greatness of His purpose.

Lord Jesus, I live for the purpose of knowing You. Amen.

Day 57

Holiness and Power

*But ye shall receive power, after the Holy
Ghost is come upon you.*

—ACTS 1:8

NOT LONG AGO I stood before great audiences of the churchmen of the world.
Someone said, "Do you not think it would be
better if the church was calling for holiness
instead of power?"

And I replied, "She will never obtain the
one without the other. There is something
larger than holiness. It is the nature of God."

The nature of God has many sides. From
every angle that the soul approaches God, a
new and different aspect of God is revealed:
love, beauty, tenderness, healing, power,
might, and wisdom.

The Christian who hungers and lifts his
soul to God, brings God down to meet his
own cry. The spirit of man and the Spirit of

God unite. The nature of God is reproduced in man.

> *God, manifest Your Spirit and power*
> *in my life. Amen.*

Day 58

Fear Not

Fear not: for I am with thee: I will bring thy seed from the east, and gather thee from the west.

—ISAIAH 43:5

HY IS IT that we do not fear? God gives us four reasons in Isaiah 43:1–7:

1. *I have redeemed thee, I have called thee by thy name; thou art mine.*

The fact He has purchased us with His precious blood should be enough to guarantee every blessing we need. He will freely give us all things (Rom. 8:32). After Calvary, anything. We are His property. He will take care of His property.

2. *He promises to go with us through the waters and the fires.*

In the dark hour we know His consolations. "Thou hast known my soul in adversities" (Ps. 31:7). The consolation of God far outweighs the pressure of our troubles.

3. *He will fulfill His plans for us in the midst of adversity.*

There is a suggestion here that God knows the infinite pain and trouble we will face. He is not likely to fail us. Nothing can work against His will.

4. *He promises spiritual fruit.*

The seed we sow may seem to perish, but we shall all come rejoicing bringing, our sheaves with us.

Jesus, Your perfect love for me removes my every fear and shatters my every anxiety. Amen.

Day 59

We Have No Fear

*Fear not; for thou shalt not be ashamed:
neither be thou confounded; for thou
shalt not be put to shame.*

—ISAIAH 54:4

ISAIAH 54:4–17 reveals four great reasons
why we have no fear:

1. *His love for His own.*

"Thy Maker is thine husband" (Isa. 54:5).
The husband cherishes his wife even at the
cost of his own life. The love of a true wife is
stronger than death.

2. *His covenant and oath.*

"So have I sworn that I would not be wroth
with thee, nor rebuke thee" (54:9). Many
Christians are under the law, and they look to
God expecting His frown or a blow. We
should live in such perfect love that we could

not imagine His displeasure.

3. *His protecting care.*

He wants our spirit, soul, and body to be preserved blameless unto His coming (1 Thess. 5:23). It simply means God will protect us from all the sicknesses and crippling diseases of the devil.

4. *His own righteousness.*

Jesus is made unto us righteousness (1 Cor. 1:30). We receive the gift of righteousness (Rom. 5:17). Who shall have anything to the charge of God's elect? It is God that justifieth (Rom. 8:33).

> *Lord, eradicate shame from my life that I may not bring shame to the gospel. Amen.*

Getting Free From Fear

There is no fear in love; but perfect love casteth out fear: because fear hath torment.

—1 JOHN 4:18

THESE ARE three considerations that will help rid us of "the fear that torments."

1. *The devil's fears are always falsehoods.*

His suggestions are always lies, and if lies, they cannot harm. If fear comes from Satan, then we can conclude there is nothing to fear.

2. *Fear is dangerous.*

It turns into fact the things we fear. It creates evil just as faith creates good.

3. *The remedy for fear is faith and love.*

"Perfect love casteth out fear" (1 John 4:17–18). "Herein is our love made perfect, that we may have boldness in the day of judgment, because as he is, so are we in this world" (1 John 4:16). Love is made perfect because we dwell in Him, who is Love.

> *In You, Lord Jesus, I have no one or no thing to fear. Amen.*

Day 61

Christ's Fullness in Us

*Till we all come in the unity of the faith,
and of the knowledge of the Son of God,
unto a perfect man, unto the measure of
the stature of the fullness of Christ.*
—EPHESIANS 4:13

EXPERIMENTALLY I knew God as Savior from sin, I knew the power of the Christ within my own heart to keep me above the power of temptation and to help me live a godly life. But when the purpose of God in the salvation of man first dawned upon my soul, that is, when the greatness of it dawned upon my soul, life became for me a grand, new thing.

By the study of God's Word, and by the revelation of His Spirit, it became a fact in my soul that God's purpose was no less in me than it was in the Lord Jesus. His purpose is no less in you and I, as younger brethren, than it was in Jesus Christ, our elder brother. Then I saw the purpose that God had in mind for the human race. Then I saw the greatness of Jesus' desire. That desire that was so intense it caused Him, as King of Glory, to lay down all that glory possessed for Him, and come to earth to be born as a man. He joined hands with our humanity, and by His grace lifts us in consciousness and life to the same level that He Himself enjoyed.

Christ became a new factor in my soul. A vision of His purpose thrilled my being. I could understand then how Jesus approached man and his needs at the very bottom, calling mankind to Him. Then by His loving touch and the power of the Spirit through His word, He destroyed the sickness and sin that bound man and set us free both in body and in soul.

My prayer, Lord Jesus, is all of You in all of me, Your fullness in me. Amen.

Day 62

The Vision of the Divine Reality

Then the eyes of the blind shall be opened,
and the ears of the deaf shall be unstopped.
Then shall the lame man leap as a hart,
and the tongue of the dumb sing.

—ISAIAH 35:5–6

I CAN UNDERSTAND the thrill that must have moved David when he sang the 103rd Psalm: "Bless the Lord, O my soul, and forget not all his benefits: who forgiveth all thine iniquities; Who healeth all thy diseases" (Ps. 103:2–3).

The vision that has called forth the shouts of praise from the souls of men in all ages is the same vision that stirs your heart and mine today. It is the vision of the divine reality of the salvation of Jesus Christ, by which the greatness of God's purpose in Him is revealed to mankind, by the Spirit of the Living One. By that great salvation we are transformed, lifted, and unified with the living Christ through the Holy Ghost, so that all the parts, energies, and functions of the nature of Jesus Christ are revealed through man unto the salvation of the world.

The vision of God's relation to man and man's relation to God is changing the character of Christianity from a groveling something, weeping and wailing its way in tears, to the kingly recognition of union and communion with the living one of God.

I am glad, bless God, that the Scriptures have dignified us with that marvelous title of "sons of God" (John 1:12). I am glad there is such a relation as a "Son of God," and that by His grace the soul is cleansed by the precious blood of Jesus Christ, filled, and energized by His own kingly Spirit. By the grace of God a saved person has become God's king, God's gentleman in deed and in truth.

> *I praise You, Lord Jesus, for imparting Your royalty to my nature. In You, I am royalty—a child of the King. Amen.*

Day 63

Christ Taking Possession of Me

I will greatly rejoice in the Lord, my soul shall be joyful in my God; for he hath clothed me with the garments of salvation.
—ISAIAH 61:10

THE SPIRIT of God is a force that takes possession of the nature of man and works in man the will of God. The will of God is ever to make man like Himself. Blessed be His precious Name.

It would be a strange Word indeed, and a strange salvation if Jesus was not able to produce from the whole race one man in His own image, in His own likeness, and of His own character. We would think that salvation was weak, would we not?

If the world were nothing but cripples, as it largely is, soul cripples, physical cripples, mental cripples everywhere, then I want to know what kind of a conception the world has received of the divinity of Jesus Christ, of the

Power of His salvation? Is there no hope, is there no way out of the difficulty, is there no force that can lift the soul of man into union with God, so that once again the life of God thrills in his members?

The mere fact of a brother's deliverance from suffering and inability to help himself, and a possible premature death, is a very small matter in itself in comparison with the wonder it reveals to us. The revelation of the power of God at the command of man, to be applied to the destruction of evil, whether spiritual or physical, mental or psychological, shows us Christ's purpose and desire to bring man by the grace of God once more into his heavenly estate, where he recognizes himself a son of God. Blessed be His Name.

How I rejoice, O Lord, that You are transforming me into Your image. Amen.

Day 64

Enter Into His Nature

*That ye, being rooted and grounded in
love, may be able to comprehend . . . what
is the breadth, and length, and depth, and
height; and to know the love of Christ.*
—EPHESIANS 3:17–19

THE SPIRIT of the Lord speaks within my
soul and says: "Within the breast of every
man is the divine image of God (living God),
in whose image and likeness he was made. Sin
is a perversion, and sickness an impostor, and
the grace and power of God through the Holy
Ghost delivers man from all bondage of darkness. Man in all his nature rises into union
and communion with God and becomes one
with Him in the truest sense."

So the divine realities remain. The reality of
God—a living power. The divine assistance,
the heavenly nature, known to every man who
enters by the Spirit through the door, Christ
Jesus, into a living experience. The man who
doubts is the man on the outside.

The man on the inside has not questions to settle that do not comprehend God, as that soul that has never been in contact with His life and power. But Christ invites mankind to enter with Him into the divine knowledge and heavenly union that makes the spirit of man and the Spirit of God one.

> *Help me, Lord, to comprehend the breadth, length, depth, and height of Your Love. Amen.*

Day 65

Growing in Christ

For which cause we faint not; but though our outward man perish, yet the inward man is renewed day by day.
—2 CORINTHIANS 4:16

SALVATION TO my heart is Christ's glorious reality. Under a tree away back in Canada one night I knelt and poured out my heart to God and asked Him by His grace to take possession of my life and nature and make me a Christian man, and let me know the power of His salvation. And Christ was born in my soul. Such a joy of God possessed my heart that the leaves of the trees seemed to dance for months following, and the birds sang a new song.

Salvation is a progressive condition. The difficulty with the church has been that men were induced to confess their sins to Christ and acknowledge Him as a Savior, and there they stopped, there they petrified, there they withered, there they died—dry-rotted. I believe in these phases I have expressed the real thing that has taken place in 85 percent of professing Christians in the world. Oh, bless God, we never saw Christ's intention.

Yea, bless God, there came a day when God once more in His loving mercy endowed me with the Spirit of God, to be and perform the things that He had planted in my soul and had revealed in His own blessed Word and life.

I invite you to this life of divine reality. I invite you to enter into the Lord Jesus. I invite you to enter into His nature that you may know Him, for no man can say that Jesus is the Lord, but by the Holy Ghost.

Change me daily, Lord, that I might grow and be renewed. Amen.

Day 66

Give!

Give, and it shall be given unto you; good measure, pressed down, and shaken together, and running over, shall men give into your bosom.

—LUKE 6:38

SO THE CHRISTIAN draws to himself the love of men, not because he slavishly desires it, but because of the fact that he obeys Christ's command to give.

And I want to tell you that this little church is one of the most loved of all churches in the world. I want to tell you that more hungry hearts are turned in longing toward this little company of people than to any other company of worshipers in the land. Why? They have heard that God is here, and the longing nature of man to know God causes them to turn their hearts and their faces toward the source of heavenly blessing. Shall we give it to them, or will they turn away hungry and dissatisfied? Yea, I know your answer, for I know the answer of the Spirit, "Give and it shall be given unto you." Blessed be God.

The greatest giver is the greatest receiver. He who gives most receives most. That is God's divine law. The reverse of God's law is always evidenced in the soul of man as selfishness. Always getting, always getting, until the nature contracts and the face distorts, and the brain diminishes, and the life that God gave to be abundant becomes an abomination that men are compelled to endure.

God, make of me a giver like You.
Amen.

Day 67

The Heart's Treasure

For where your treasure is, there will your heart be also.

—MATTHEW 6:21

A LADY CAME into this audience for the first time, got under conviction, was saved, and gave her heart to God. Three days later, she was sanctified by the precious blood of Jesus, and on Friday night she was baptized in the Holy Ghost. After the service, I talked to her for a few moments. She said, "Oh, Brother, if I could just tell you the delights of my soul during these last thirty-six hours. If I could only explain how my spirit has found a freedom in God and how it seems to me my heart would rush to Him."

Where is your treasure? In heaven, bless God! Well, you will go where your treasure is.

My heart's treasure is You, Lord Jesus. Amen.

Heavenly Knowledge

*But God hath chosen the foolish things of
the world to confound the wise; and God
hath chosen the weak things of the world
to confound the things which are mighty.*
—1 CORINTHIANS 1:27

AFTER A NIGHT of talking with a group of
great intellectuals in their office, I said,
"Dear God, it is absolutely impossible to make
an unenlightened, unsaved soul to understand
the difference between the Spirit of God and
every other spirit. The Spirit of God is the
attractive power that animates the Christian
heart, and they do not want to listen to anything else." Jesus said, "[My sheep] know My
voice" (see John 10:41).

I left there next morning with profound
sympathy in my heart. I said as I walked away,
"Dear God, here are the greatest intellects in
the world, but concerning the things of God
and the light of the Spirit they are just as blind
as though their eyes were sealed."

Men come in the name of science. Naturally there is a certain reverence for knowledge, but don't be fooled. Just because somebody comes along with the light of worldly knowledge, no matter how minute and wonderful it may seem, the knowledge he has is worldly; the knowledge *you* have is heavenly. The knowledge that his soul possesses is material; the knowledge that *your* soul possesses is divinely spiritual. It comes from the heart of God.

*Christ, fill my mind and heart with
Your knowledge. Amen.*

Avoid Spiritualism

*And when they shall say unto you, Seek
unto them that have familiar spirits, and
unto wizards that peep, and that mutter:
should not a people seek unto their God?*
—Isaiah 8:19

THERE IS ONE source of knowledge; that is
God. This Word of God does not even
give me the privilege of seeking guidance of
angels, let alone from the spirit of the dead or
the spirit of a living man. It gives me one privilege. There is One Mind that knows all, that
is the mind of God, and if I am His child, and
if my heart is made pure by the blood of His
Son, then I have a right to come into His presence and secure anything my heart may want.

*All I need to know, all the wisdom I
desire, is in You, Lord Jesus. Amen.*

Day 70

Only in Christ Is There Life

In him was life; and the life was the light of men.

—JOHN 1:4

DO YOU KNOW we do not read the Scriptures like people read a textbook. Have you ever observed how a scientist reads his textbook? He weighs every single word, and each word has a peculiar meaning.

If we read the Word of God like that we would get the real vitality of what it says. I wonder if we have caught the force of this Scripture: "Paul, an apostle of Jesus Christ by the will of God, according to the promise of life which is in Christ Jesus" (2 Tim. 1:1).

There is no life outside of Jesus Christ, no eternal life outside of Jesus Christ, by the declaration of Jesus Himself. John said: "God hath given to us eternal life, and this life is in his Son. He that hath the Son hath life; and he that hath not the Son of God hath not life" (1 John 5:11–12).

Observe these words: "According to the promise of life." There is no promise of life outside of Jesus Christ. Jesus was the most emphatic teacher the world ever saw. He said: "Ye must be born again" (John 3:7). There is no arbitration by which you can get around the matter. There is no possibility of avoiding that truth. You have got to come straight to it and meet it. "According to the promise of life which is in Christ Jesus."

> *Jesus, I confess that in You alone is life. Amen.*

Day 71

The Word of God

All scripture is given by inspiration of God, and is profitable for doctrine, for reproof, for correction, for instruction in righteousness.

—2 Timothy 3:16

ALL THE SCRIPTURES are dear to my heart, and bring their peculiar ministry and lesson, but the words of Jesus are the supreme words of the gospel. Jesus said: "It is the spirit that quickeneth . . . the words that I speak unto you, they are spirit, and they are life" (John 6:63). Do you know the difficulty in our day is that we have run away from Jesus. That is, the church at large has. The world is making a great struggle at the present hour to get back to Jesus, and we are in the midst of it ourselves.

We have run into false theology, we have run into "churchianity" and human interpretations, and a hundred other follies, but friends, it is a perfectly lovely and refreshing thing to get back to Jesus. Take the words of Jesus and let them become the supreme court of the gospel to you.

I consider all the Word of God the common court of the gospel, but the words of Jesus are the supreme court of the gospel. If there is a question that is not clearly decided according to your vision in the common court of the gospel, then refer it to the supreme court, and the words of Jesus will settle anything that is in your mind.

If our questions were settled by the words of Jesus, we would be out of all the confusion that the world is in at present. I do not see any other way for the world to come out of her present confusion unless it is to accept the words of Jesus as final authority, to accept Jesus as the divine finality where all questions are finally adjudicated.

> *Your Word, O God, is the final authority of my life. Amen.*

Stir Up The Gift In You

*Wherefore I put thee in remembrance
that thou stir up the gift of God, which is
in thee by the putting on of my hands.*
—2 Timothy 1:6

AUL HAD some faith in the value of the putting on of his hands. It was not a mere form. I want to call your attention to the Word of God especially on this line. Paul's own convictions were that through laying on of hands upon this young man, an impartation of God to his life had been given.

It was so real that even though Timothy was not aware of it and was not exercising the power of God thus bestowed, yet Paul's conviction was that the power of God was present. Why? Because he had laid his hands on Timothy in the name of the Lord Jesus Christ, and he believed the Spirit of the Lord Jesus Christ had been imparted to Timothy. Therefore the gift of God was in him.

Beloved, it takes faith to exercise your gift of God. There are just lots of people around everywhere who have gifts of God, and they are lying dormant in their lives, and there is no value for the kingdom of God through them because they have no faith in God to put the gift in exercise and get the benefit of it.

Too many preachers are afraid of the devil. They have no idea how big God is. They preach fear of the devil, fear of demons, fear of this influence, fear of that influence, and fear of some other power. If the Holy Ghost has come down from heaven into your soul, common sense teaches that He has made you the master thereby of every other power in the world. Otherwise the Word of God is a blank falsehood. For it declares: "Greater is he that is in you, than he that is in the world" (1 John 4:4).

> *Lord, give me the courage to use the gift that You have put in me. Amen.*

Day 73

Casting Out Devils

*And these signs shall follow those who
believe; In my name shall they cast out
devils; they shall speak with new tongues.*
—MARK 16:17

I TALKED AT A conference in Africa about
the matter of devils. I said, "It is a strange
thing to me that in all the years of missions in
this land, that your hands are tied on account
of witch doctors. Why don't you go out and
cast the devil out of these fellows, and get the
people delivered from their power?"

The secret of our work, the reason God
gave us one hundred thousand people, the
reason we have more than twelve hundred
native preachers in our work in Africa, is
because of the fact we believed the promise:
"Greater is he that is in you, than he that is in
the world" (1 John 4:4).

We not only went to seek them, but chal-
lenged them separately and united, and by the

power of God delivered the people from their power. When they were delivered, the people appreciated their deliverance from the slavery in which they had been held through their superstitions and psychological spirit control, and they are most terrible. "God hath not given us the spirit of fear; but of power, and of love, and of a sound mind" (2 Tim. 1:7).

Lord, give me Your eyes that I might see the spiritual realities around me. Amen.

Day 74

He That Is in You

Greater is he that is in you, than he that is in the world.

—1 John 4:4

GOD ANOINTS your soul. God anoints your life. God comes to dwell in your person. God comes to make you a master. That is the purpose of His indwelling in a Christian. The real child of God was to be a master over every other power of darkness in the world. The world was to be subject to him. He is to be God's representative in the world.

The Holy Ghost in the Christian was to be as powerful as the Holy Ghost was in Christ. Indeed, Jesus' words go to such an extreme that they declare: "Greater works than these shall he do" (John 14:12). It indicates that the mighty Holy Ghost from heaven in the life of the Christian was to be more powerful in you and in me after Jesus got to heaven and ministered Him to our souls, than He was in Jesus.

Fear of the devil is nonsense. Fear of demons is foolish. The Spirit of God anointing the Christian heart makes the soul impregnable to the powers of darkness.

"God hath not given us the spirit of fear, but of power, and of love, and of a sound mind." (2 Tim. 1:7). The Spirit of power is the Holy Ghost, bless God. And not only of power, but of love and of a sound mind. Not a craziness and insanity, but a sound mind by which you can look in the face of the devil and laugh.

Lord, I thank You that the Holy Spirit gives me power over the devil and all his demons. Amen.

Day 75

Be an Overcomer

And they overcame him [the accuser] by
the blood of the Lamb.
—REVELATION 12:11

IN THE JEWISH Bible, among the listings of
the covenants, is the one that is known as
the Threshold Covenant. That was the
Covenant by which the Israelites went out of
the land of Egypt, when God told them to slay
a lamb, and put the blood on the doorposts
and lintel. And the Jewish Bible adds by
saying that they put the blood on the
threshold. A lot of people get the blood of
Jesus on their head, but it seems to me they do
not get it under their feet.

The Word of God teaches us to get the
blood under your feet, and on the right hand
and on the left hand and over your head. That
is your protection. There was no angel of
death in the land of Egypt, or in hell, that

could go through the blood unto that family. No Sir! He was absolutely barred.

Friends, do you believe it was the blood of the lamb that was barring the angel of death? Do you believe the red stains on the doors frightened him away? No, the blood signified to me that there is one that goes through the blood; that is the Holy Ghost. And, beloved, the Eternal God by the Spirit went through the blood to the inside, and stayed there and defended the house.

I am sure of one thing, if Christianity was to leave me a weakling to be oppressed by the power of darkness, I would seek something else, because it would not meet my need. It is that which meets the need that gives you divine supremacy in Jesus Christ.

Lord Jesus, by Your Spirit I apply the blood to my life, my family, and all that I have. Amen.

Day 76

The Indwelling Christ

When he [Jesus] had called unto him his
twelve disciples, he gave them the power. . . .
—MATTHEW 10:1

BELOVED, HE gives it to you. What is the
Holy Ghost? It is the gift of God
Himself to you. The Holy Spirit is not simply
given that you may be a channel, and always a
channel. No Sir! The most magnificent thing
the Word of God portrays is that Christ,
indwelling in you by the Holy Ghost, makes
you a son of God like Jesus Christ, with the
recognized power of God in your spirit to
command the will of God.

It may not be that all souls have grown to
that place where such a life as that is evident,
but surely if the Son of God by the Holy
Ghost has been born in our heart, it is time we
began to let Him have some degree of sway in
our heart, and some degree of heavenly

dominion of value, and some degree of the lightnings of Jesus Christ breaking forth from our spirit.

The sanest man is the man who believes God and stands on His promises, knows the secret of His power, receives the Holy Ghost, gives Him sway in his life, and goes out in the name of the Lord Jesus to command the will of God and bring it to pass in the world.

> *Spirit of God, use me to set others free from the powers of sickness and unclean spirits through the name of Jesus. Amen.*

The Prayer of Faith

*The prayer of faith shall save the sick,
and the Lord shall raise him up.*
—James 5:15

THE PRAYER of faith has power. The prayer of faith has trust. The prayer of faith has healing for soul and body. The disciples wanted to know how to pray real prayers, and Jesus said unto them, "When ye pray, say, Our Father which art in heaven . . . Thy will be done" (Luke 11:2).

Everybody stops there—at "Thy will be done"—and they resign their intelligence at that point to the unknown God. When you approach people and say to them, "You have missed the spirit of prayer," they look at you in amazement. But, beloved, it is a fact I want to show to you this afternoon as it is written in the Word of God. It does not say, "If it be thy will" and stop there. There is a comma there, not a period. The prayer is this, "Thy will be done, as in heaven, so in earth" (Luke 11:2). That is a mite different, is it not? Not, "Thy will be done. Let the calamity come. Let my children be stricken with fever, or my son go to the insane asylum, or my daughter go to the home of the feeble-minded."

That is not what Jesus was teaching the people to pray. Jesus was teaching the people to pray, "Thy will be done on earth as it is in heaven." Let the might of God be known. Let the power of God descend. Let God avert the calamity that is coming. Let it turn aside through faith in God. "Thy will be done on earth as it is in heaven."

Father, may Your will be done in my life as it is in heaven. Amen.

Day 78

Believing, Pray for Healing

When ye pray, believe that ye receive them, and ye shall have them.

—MARK 11:24

THERE IS NO question in the mind of God concerning the salvation of a sinner. No more is there question concerning the healing of the sick one. It is in the atonement of Jesus Christ, bless God. His atonement was unto the uttermost; to the last need of man.

The responsibility rests purely, solely, and entirely on man. Jesus put it there. Jesus said, "When ye pray, believe that ye receive them, and *ye shall have them.*" No questions, or "ifs," in the words of Jesus. If He ever spoke with emphasis on any question, it was on the subject of God's will and the result of faith in prayer. Indeed, He did not even speak them in ordinary words, but in the custom of the East. He said, "Verily, verily." Amen, amen—the same as if I were to stand in an American court and say, "I swear to tell the truth, the whole truth, and nothing but the truth, so help me God."

So the Easterner raised his hand and said, "Amen, amen," or "Verily, verily"—"with the solemnity of an oath I say unto you."

So instead of praying, "Lord, if it be Thy will" when you kneel beside your sick friend, Jesus Christ has commanded you and every believer, lay your hands on the sick. This is not my ministry nor my brethren's only. It is the ministry of every believer. And if your ministers do not believe it, God have mercy on them. If your churches do not believe it, God have mercy on them.

Lord, give me the boldness to pray for all the sick that I meet, believing Your will for their healing. Amen.

Day 79

The Holy Spirit

And Jesus returned in the power of the Spirit.

—LUKE 4:14

IF WE STUDY the manner by which the Spirit of God revealed Himself through Jesus, then we will have the pattern or example of how the Spirit of God reveals Himself through all believers all the time.

Through His nature there flowed a subtle power that no religionist but Himself and His followers possessed—the living Spirit of the living God, the anointing of the Holy Ghost.

So long as Christianity is dependent on the presence of the Holy Ghost it will remain distinctively the one religion of divine power and saving grace.

Holy Spirit, my life depends totally on You. Amen.

A Pure Heart

Flee also youthful lusts: but follow righteousness, faith, charity, peace, with them that call on the Lord out of a pure heart.
—2 TIMOTHY 2:22

WHEN A YOUNG MAN, I stood in an aisle of the Methodist Church and was introduced to a young lady. As I touched her hand, the marvelous moving of our natures was revealed. Presently something from her soul, that subtle something that Christians know and recognize as spirit, her spirit passed to me, went through my person until presently I realized that my soul had rent itself in affection for that woman, and we never had looked into each other's eyes in an intimate way before. From me went that subtle something to her. The result was that we were just as much soul mates and lovers in the next ten minutes as we were in the next seventeen years of raising a family.

She was a woman of fine sensitive qualities, and she told me later that she had been in the habit of searching a young man's spirit to know if he was pure; but, she said, "In your case, the strange thing was, that my spirit made no such search. I just knew it."

I want to tell you in that matter she was not wrong, for when I was a boy, though I was surrounded by as vile a set of men as have ever lived, I determined in my soul that one day I would look into a woman's soul and tell her that I was pure.

If you held the hand of Jesus right now, do you suppose your spirit would be capable of searching His soul to know whether He was pure?

Suppose the Spirit of Jesus searched your soul, would He discern purity? What would the Spirit of Jesus discern in you? What would He discern in me?

Create in me, O God, a pure heart.
Amen.

Day 81

The Christian's Offering

My son, give me thine heart, and let thine eyes observe my ways.
—PROVERBS 23:26

WE COME, not with a dove, or a lamb, or a he goat, or a heifer. No, we come with our all, offering it to the Lord. Not bargaining with Him to obtain the blessing.

Very rarely have I known people to miss the blessing of God when they came openly, saying, "I desire to receive; I want to give." That is the secret of all affection between man and man, between the sexes. Men are not always seeking for someone to love them; they are seeking for someone that they can love.

When two souls are seeking for the one they can love, there is a union, and the world very gradually is learning that there are real marriages. There is a union of spirit so indissoluble that nothing on earth or in heaven will ever sunder them.

Christ is seeking for the soul that will receive His love, and the Christian, the real one, is seeking for the Christ who will receive his love. Both are practicing the unalterable law of God, "Give, and it shall be given unto you."

Christ is seeking the affection of mankind, for without their affection there can never be that deep union of the spirit between God and man that makes possible a richness of life, made glorious by His indwelling.

You can give to your Lord your money, your property, your brain, and all the other things that are usually considered to be very excellent, but if you withhold your affections from Him and give them to another, the Word says you are an adulterer.

Our Father, teach us to love You.
Amen.

Day 82

The Peace of God

*And the peace of God, which passeth all
understanding, shall keep your hearts
and minds through Christ Jesus.*
—PHILIPPIANS 4:7

WHEN THE SOULS of men learn to rest in
confidence upon the living God, peace
will possess this world and it will be like unto
the kingdom of God—heaven on earth.

Most of our difficulties are those we antici-
pate or fear will come tomorrow. How many
people are worrying about the things of today?
But the world is in consternation concerning
tomorrow, or the next day, or the next day.
Jesus said, "Sufficient unto the day is the evil
thereof" (Matt. 6:34). Do not worry about
tomorrow. Rest in God. The mighty arms of
the living God will be underneath tomorrow,
just as they are today.

The Spirit of God says within my heart that
the kingdom of Christ, for which every child

of God looks, is characterized by the peace of God possessing the souls of men, so that worry and care cease to be because we trust in His arms.

If I could bring to you today one blessing greater than another, it would be the consciousness of trust in God. "Be not afraid, neither be thou dismayed: for the Lord thy God is with thee whithersoever thou goest" (Josh. 1:9).

Lord, guard my heart with Your peace. May I always be able to say, O my soul, be not afraid, for wherever I go, the Lord goes with me. Amen.

Day 83

Sufficient for Every Need

Not that we are sufficient of ourselves to think any thing as of ourselves; but our sufficiency is of God.

—2 CORINTHIANS 3:5

THE LIFE of God, the Spirit of God, the nature of God are sufficient for every need of man. In the highest sense of the word, he is a real Christian whose body, soul, and spirit alike are filled with the Life of God.

The object of healing is health, abiding health of body, soul, and spirit. The healing of the spirit unites the spirit of man to God forever. The healing of the soul corrects psychic disorders and brings the soul processes into harmony with the mind of God. And the healing of the body completes the union of man with God when the Holy Spirit possesses all.

Jesus, my sufficiency of body, soul, and spirit rests solely in You. Amen.

Lay Hold of God

*Fear not, Daniel: for from the first day
that thou didst set thine heart to understand . . . thy words were heard, and I
am come for thy words.*

—DANIEL 10:12

SOMETIMES YOU have to lay hold of God,
and stay before God, and stay through
the blackness and through the darkness and
through the night of it, until the faith of God
penetrates, and the work is done.

Do you remember the experience of Daniel,
one of the finest in the Book? He had to hear
from heaven. He fasted and prayed for
twenty-one days. On the twenty-first day, an
angel came to him and said, "Daniel, a man
greatly beloved . . . from the first day . . . thy
words were heard." Not the last time you
prayed, but the very first.

"But the prince of the kingdom of Persia
withstood me one and twenty days: but, lo,
Michael, one of the chief princes, came to

help me; and I remained there with the kings of Persia. Now I am come to make thee understand what shall befall thy people in the latter days" (Dan. 10:13–14).

Michael is spoken of again as the warrior angel. He made way against the devil and cast him out of heaven. Daniel had prayed, and God heard his prayer and answered it by sending an angel messenger, but the messenger himself was held up on the way by some other power of darkness until reinforcements came and God dispatched "Michael" to help.

You are praying. Beloved, have you faith in God to stay and pray until the Spirit has a chance to work out the problem? That is the issue. Keep right down to it. Do not let go. It is the will of God; you have a right it.

Almighty God, give me strength to lay hold of You and never let go. Amen.

Day 85

Cleansed by the Spirit

And such were some of you: but ye are washed, but ye are sanctified, but ye are justified in the name of the Lord Jesus, and by the Spirit of our God.
—1 CORINTHIANS 6:11

THE SPIRIT never comes to a man's life to whitewash him over or smooth him over or clean him up. God comes to him to make him new and give him a new heart. God gives him a new mind, a new spirit, new blood, new bone, and new flesh.

God's Spirit sends him out with a new song in his mouth, and a new shout of praise in his heart, and a new realization of holiness—a truly *redeemed* man.

God, fill us by Your Spirit, and send us forth among men—not whitewashed, but washed white with your God's grace. Amen.

Total Commitment

And the very God of peace sanctify you
wholly; and I pray God your whole spirit
and soul and body be preserved blameless
unto the coming of our Lord Jesus Christ.
—1 THESSALONIANS 5:23

FIRST COMMIT your body and soul and spirit in entire, hundredfold consecration to God forever. Do not be satisfied with sins forgiven.

Press on, press in, let God have you and fill you, until consciously He dwells, lives, abides in every cell of your blood, your bone, and your brain; until your soul, indwelt by Him, thinks His thoughts, speaks His Word; until your spirit assimilates God, and God's Spirit assimilates you; until your humanity and His divinity are merged into His eternal Deity.

Thus body, soul, and spirit are God's forever.

Lord, fill every fiber of my being with
Your Holy Spirit. Amen.

Day 87

Divine Healing

For I am the Lord that healeth thee.
                                        —EXODUS 15:26

IN DIVINE HEALING today, the unchangeableness of God's eternal purpose is thereby demonstrated. "Jesus Christ the same yesterday, and today and for ever" (Heb. 13:8). "I am the Lord, I change not" (Mal. 3:6).

God always was the healer. He is the healer still, and will ever remain the healer. Healing is for you. Jesus healed all that came to Him. He never turned anyone away. He never said: "It is not God's will to heal you," or that it was better for the individual to remain sick, or that they were being perfected in character through the sickness.

Jesus healed them all, thereby demonstrating forever God's unchangeable will concerning sickness and healing.

Have you need of healing? Pray to God in the Name of Jesus Christ to remove the disease. Command it to leave you, as you would sin. Assert your divine authority, and refuse to have it. Jesus purchased your freedom from sickness as He purchased your freedom from sin.

> *Jesus, by Your power and authority, I am healed. Amen.*

By His Stripes

*Who own self bare our sins in his own
body on the tree, that we, being dead to
sins, should live unto righteousness: by
whose stripes ye were healed.*

—1 PETER 2:24

THEREFORE, humanity has a right to
health, as we has a right to deliverance
from sin. If you do not have it, it is because
you are being cheated out of your inheritance.
It belongs to you in the name of Jesus Christ.
Go after it and get it.

If your faith is weak, call for those who
believe, and to whom the prayer of faith and
the ministry of healing has been committed.

Sin, sickness, and death are doomed—
doomed to death by the decree of Christ Jesus.
Sin, sickness, and death are the triumvirate of
the devil. The triple curse. Heaven is the
absence of this triple curse—heaven is sinless-
ness, health, and eternal life.

Jesus anticipated the world's need and your

need. He commanded His power for the use of humanity.

He invites you to help yourself to His eternal quality and become, thereby, the sons of God.

> *I come to You, Lord Jesus, for all that You have for me—forgiveness of sin, health, and eternal life. Amen.*

Day 89

In His Name

Whatsoever ye shall ask the Father in my name, he will give it you.

—John 16:23

MATCHLESS NAME! The secret of power was in it. When the disciples used the name the power struck. The dynamite of heaven exploded.

Peter and John were hustled off to jail. The church prayed for them "in the name." They were released. They went to the church. The entire church prayed that signs and wonders might be done. How did they pray? In "the name." They used it legally. The vital response was instantaneous. The place was shaken as by an earthquake. Tremendous name!

Jesus commanded: "Go into all the world." Why? To proclaim the name. To use the name. In it was concentrated the combined authority resident in the Father, the Son, and the Holy Ghost.

The apostles used the name. It worked. The deacons at Samaria used the name. The fire flashed. Believers everywhere, forever, were commanded to use it. The name detonated around the world.

Prayer in His name gets answers. The Moravians prayed. The greatest revival till that time hit the world. Finney prayed. America rocked with power. Hudson Taylor prayed. China's Inland Mission was born. Evan Roberts prayed seven years. The Welsh revival resulted.

Pray in the name of Jesus!

> *In Your name, Lord Jesus, I pray for the fire of Your Holy Spirit to baptize me. Amen.*

Day 90

A Prayer for the Inner Life

*For this cause I bow my knees unto the
Father of our Lord Jesus Christ . . . that he
would grant you . . . to be strengthened
with might by his Spirit in the inner man.*
—EPHESIANS 3:14, 16

MY GOD, we bless Thee for the ideal of
the gospel of Christ which Thou hast
established in the souls of men through the
blessed Holy Ghost. God, we pray Thee this
afternoon that if we have thought lightly of
the Spirit of God, if we have had our eyes
fixed on outward evidences instead of the
inward life, we pray Thee to sweep it away
from our souls.

May we this day, God, see indeed that the
life of God—His Life in our inner selves
revealed by Christ's perfect life—is to be
revealed in us. May the Lord Jesus through us
shed forth His glory, life, benediction, peace,
and power upon the world. Blessed be Thy
precious Name.

So my God, we open our nature to heaven today, asking that the Spirit of the living God will thus move in our own soul, that by His grace we shall be so perfectly, truly cleansed of God that our nature will be sweet, pure, heavenly, and true.

We desire to receive from God the blessed sweetness of His pure, holy, heavenly Spirit to reign in us, to rule over us, to control us, and to guide us forevermore. Amen.

Amen.